Enlightenment Now

The Keys to Awakening

G. Tyler Wright

Enlightenment Now

TranscendentWritings.com

Contents

Preface

Is the title of this book accurate, or is it maybe just a little overly ambitious? You are the ultimate judge, but enlightenment only takes a moment, and each moment is only a "now", so yes, I believe *Enlightenment Now* is exactly what happens to each of us at the penultimate point of our spiritual journey. If you can empower yourself to believe your "now" has arrived, then any instant can be your instant.

The title of my last book was *How to Become Enlightened in 12 Days*, and I received many interesting comments on the title including one stating, "It does not take 12 days to become enlightened." I know this to be true, but I also know the human mind needs to have structure and foundation before it can begin to form new belief. Focusing for 12 days using exercises designed specifically to expand the self beyond the previously believed confines of the mind is for some a sufficient time for the breakthrough known as enlightenment.

I also realized for some seekers, 12 days to reach the ultimate understanding seemed insufficient, and for those, I have written *Enlightenment Now: The Keys to Awakening*. This book takes a longer view of the process of enlightenment, and is formatted in a different way to assist those who need more information. The best lessons come from personal experience, and in these pages you will find my experiences, and my synthesis of these experiences into the choice of a path that best fits you.

Your chosen path will take you to your experience of enlightenment at the pace with which you are most comfortable.

This book begins with a look at what enlightenment really is, and how we can attain it. We look at this world, our place in it. We start by holding a mirror to our self and coming to know who this seeker we believe ourselves to be really is, and what we are really looking for. From there we go on to a deeper understanding of our ultimate goal, and how to get there.

Next we explore my experiences as a boy studying the ancient teachings of the masters. This exploration culminates after 16 years with learning the secrets to enlightenment and attaining realization. This journey to enlightenment passes through understanding and synthesizing the highest teachings from some of the most revered masters from around the world.

At this point in the journey, in the mind, there was no longer a belief in a separate me, but instead a real, live experience of living as the Self. What it means to live like this is also explored.

After that, we explore the most profound paths I experienced as a seeker. The keys to each path are shown and the engaged seeker can choose a path with which they best resonate. The engaged reader can also choose to move into the highest combination of teachings and supercharge the search, bringing it to culmination, if desired.

This book is the fruit of over 20 years of living an enlightened experience in the world as a husband, father, and working professional knowing that I was none of these, yet living as each, enjoying all, and delving ever deeper into how to share this experience with others.

These profound insights make up this book which illuminates the keys to an attainment meant for all to experience. This book will guide you to a path that works best for you in order to take you to the experience for which we all yearn, an experience that is the birthright of all, not just of monks and ascetics.

These teachings have been prepared by an enlightened householder in order to enlighten householders everywhere, for now is the time for enlightenment to be shared by all.

Introduction

Life appears as a series of moments, one running seamlessly into another throughout the course of our lives. The moment of enlightenment is another moment, but a crucial one, in the life of the mind. For the average person it is the border marking the end of being a separate individual and the beginning of being a universal being; for the seeker it is the dividing line between woeful misunderstanding and the highest wisdom. In my life, it was the end of a seemingly endless yearning, and the start of a blissful existence.

Come with me on an incredible journey and use this book as nothing more than the alarm clock a special part of you set long ago to awaken yourself when the time was at hand for your moment of enlightenment. Pause and deeply consider each section, and become an active participant, not just a reader.

If you will agree to do this, in these pages, you will hear the words, "Wake up, your moment is here and now!"

The famous Zen quote says, "Before enlightenment, chop wood, carry water. After enlightenment, chop wood, carry water." Numerous Gurus talk about the joy of continuing the practices that they did before becoming enlightened. For me, understanding and experiencing there is not a "me," not a person, but only a feeling of Self or Being deep within was life-changing. Without a doubt, one phase of life ended and another began with this realization. There was now a body and mind, living in the here and now that used to think of itself as a "me", but now the me was gone.

You can't even say, "What do I do?" because there is no I to *do* anymore, so the paradox of living takes on a whole new twist. At first when you realize there is no I that does anything, there is a great feeling of relief. Then the memory arises that dinner needs to be made, the trash needs to go out, and bed time is approaching.

The good news is that you don't have to do these things anymore because there is no you. In fact there never was a "you" doing any of these things, but only the Universe or Creation working through the body/mind or the entity that thought itself to be a "you." There was only ever the body/mind that misappropriated the feeling of Beingness or Self deep inside and made it an "I". There was never a "me" to take out the trash, to chop wood, carry water or fix dinner, and there isn't one now, so there isn't anything to worry about or to do.

So the body/mind sits and waits for the Universe to do its chores and guess what? Nothing happens. Eventually the thought arises, "Guess it's time for dinner." Looking around, there is no dinner, so the thought arises, "Time to make dinner," and the magic of Creation is set in motion.

The mind that always had considered itself me now has been given back to the Universe, so all thought is recognized as being from and part of Creation. Not just all action, but all thought too. Nothing belongs to you because there really is no you. Everything that is happening around the former you is the same as before; only the understanding of what is happening around the former you is different. And it this understanding is what obliterates the former you.

So what before was a person standing in the kitchen, looking in the refrigerator, deciding what to fix is now an aspect of the Universe, standing in the kitchen, looking in the refrigerator, deciding what to fix. Before you knew this, before this understanding, volition was a big mystery. Now that this understanding exists in the mind, it is simple. Before the thinking mind mistakenly said, "I want spaghetti tonight; I love pasta." Now thinking with correct understanding says, "The Universe here and now wants this body to eat spaghetti tonight. This body/mind has many past experiences and memories that allow the feeling of love to be connected with the thought of pasta."

Yes, a much truer statement. And oh how convoluted the language! In this book, the Universe writing this will be much more colloquial. The discerning reader has of course noticed that I have already taken a liberty in writing this using the terms you and I. In reality, there is only Creation doing all of this, not an "I" doing the writing who has experienced enlightenment and not a "you" reading this, who will one day experience enlightenment. You and I are both convenient colloquialisms that help keep this subject as simple as possible, intending to increase your understanding by doing so. I write from the perspective of enlightenment, but as a body/mind offering insight to other body/minds all of whom ultimately share the same Self.

So I want dinner, I fix dinner, I eat, I take out the garbage and go to bed, knowing all the time that it is the Universe acting through the body that is doing all of this. The play that is life is unfolding through what I formerly thought of as a little "me". No change in actions, only in understanding. I go to bed, I sit for an hour or two in meditation, as I always have done, and then I sleep. I experience the bliss of existence in a rush, see the light deep within, and experience the no thought phase, just as I did before. Only now I know this is only the Universe doing what it does best, through what I formerly thought of as me. And I know that I am the Universe.

"How did this understanding arise?" you may wonder, and "What use is it?" Oh, and most importantly, "What are the secrets to attaining Self-realization?" and "How can I experience enlightenment for myself?" you may ask. The answer to these questions and many others are contained within (this book)!

Chapter One: What Is Enlightenment?

When a topic is fraught with as much baggage and as many preconceptions as enlightenment is, it is sometimes helpful to understand what something is not before understanding what it is. If we can eliminate the trappings and meanings and wishful thinking that could otherwise cloud our understanding, then we can arrive at a useful definition from whence to proceed.

When I started my search, I thought of enlightenment as something that Jesus had. I thought it meant healing people, performing miracles, being loving towards everyone, knowing the truths of the universe and being at total inner peace every moment of life. Basically I thought if I could get it, then I would be the perfect person.

Now I understand that these abilities and understandings are things that can happen in the play of life, but they are not defining elements of enlightenment. People can become healers and do miraculous healings, but that is not what enlightenment is. That is what being a healer is, inside of the play.

Being loving towards everyone is great, but again, many preconceptions of this ideal do not fit well in the play of existence. As long as there are two people in the world, there will be two different perspectives, and that is the way the play is meant to be. We can love the essence of the person, and disagree with the action they perform. Very few have the words "love all, always," on their scripts for life, although life would change instantly if more did. Emanating love to all, approaching all with love, respecting all as fellow players in this play, appreciating that we all share the same Self, and loving this Self of all that we share… this is what is real in this life, and what we can do when we are enlightened, and even before.

Most actions we perform in life come from our own small definition of love. We must come to a place where we expand our understanding of love, and include all of Creation inside our circle of love. As long as we hold onto our tiny circle of love, behaving loving to those within the circle, doing things to support those on the inside, at the expense of those on the outside, then we do not really know an open true love, but only a selfish, self-interested love. Enlightenment opens our circle so that we know ourselves as encompassing the whole, and having an infinitely large circle of love. Who cannot love that which is their own Self?

To know the universe is again another experience in the play of life. When I had my experience of expanding to encompass the entire room, it was not an enlightenment experience, it was an experience of an altered state inside of this play. The Self permeated the experience as it permeates all experiences, but the experience itself is not indicative of enlightenment. That experience or any other one filled with light, love, majestic sounds or a vision of being pure light sitting on the right hand of God is no more an experience of enlightenment than the experience of eating a ham sandwich.

As amazing as they are, and as different from our normal experience of daily life as they may be, these experiences are still the movement of form and the action of the players on the stage of life. They are not enlightenment, but they can be used to free our minds from believing that what we see in front of us is all there is. These experiences, when understood correctly can allow the mind to open up to a higher understanding of reality, and become more accepting that who we usually think of ourselves as being could possibly be incorrect. When we use them in this light, they become stepping stones toward enlightenment. Even if we do not personally have them, if we can accept the words of others, learning from their experiences, then we can also gain the fruit of their experiences- the knowledge that we are much more than we seem to be.

To be at peace in every moment is what the Self does. It is not an experience of the mind, but instead it lies beyond thought. So essentially we all, as the Self, are always in this experience. When we use the mind to remember the Self, we remember the peace, the joy, the silent stillness that we are beyond the mind. To remember this in every moment is to see the screen at every moment while watching the movie. It can happen, but it does not have to happen.

Enlightenment is experienced through thousands of minds each of whom know it differently. Its flavor changes with each new perspective. Some are in life situations that allow remembering to occur continuously, living alone in an isolated monastery or mountaintop, while most are playing roles that are less conducive to constant remembrance of the self.

An experience inside of the play does not define one who understands and experiences the connection beyond the play.

Others definitions of one who is enlightened include a person who knows everything, a person who can do anything, a person who does everything with grace, a person who emits an aura of peace, and many other fantasy individuals. All these definitions have in common that they are a person doing something, and enlightenment has nothing to do with a person doing anything. Enlightenment is the letting go of a person altogether, not the adding of abilities to a person. It is a reaching and experiencing outside of the play, untouched by the play; it is not another role in the play.

When I first embarked on my quest for enlightenment, I held some of these misconceptions. When people said, "You can feel a peace around the Guru," I believed that this was a sign of enlightenment. When people talk about realized beings and say, "They move with grace and every action is a prayer," again I looked at this as a way to recognize enlightenment. I built many edifices for my definition of enlightenment, but ultimately they were my own personal construct, and I had to dismantle them all before I could see the doorway that led to a real enlightenment.

After years of contemplating my beliefs, I saw that many of the things seekers attribute to a realized master are actually nothing more than the trappings our minds add to actions we observe. If I see you pouring a glass of juice, I can think, "Boy I hope she doesn't spill that all over the table." I have attributed you with the possibility of being messy. I could also think, "Wow, she is pouring with such grace." Again, I have decided what is going on inside of you, and this time I have labeled it grace.

I could be sitting silently with you in a room and think, "He doesn't like me; he won't even say one word to me. He doesn't have any respect for me at all." Or I could think, "He is such a profound being, sitting in stillness without the need to utter a word. I feel a blessing emanating from him through just his gaze." Whatever fantasy I want to make up about your inner motivations, I can. And I will feel the truth of them as long as I want to believe them.

We are the ones who place the auras around the heads of the saints of the world. It is our vision that decides the peace is there, and it is our beliefs that set them far above and apart from ourselves. I used to think, "If I were alive during the lifetime of a great saint, I would certainly follow him or her." The truth is, would I even have had the eyes to recognize something special? Since there are truly no outer signs beyond what I attribute to someone, would I have listened to those around a great saint and believed and followed them, or would I have been one of the multitude of skeptics who saw nothing and believed nothing?

Each enlightened being has his or her role in this play of life. Some are the stars, others are the supporting cast, and some are the extras. This is true for all of us, enlightened and unaware alike. We play our part, and when it is our moment in the spotlight, we do the best we know how. I liken it to a rose: some of us get to be the petals of the flower, others to be the stem, and still others get to play the role of the thorns. Each player in this grand play has an equally important role, but some roles appear to be more glamourous than others. We all want to be the crowning achievement, the petals, but where would the petals be if not for the stem supplying the nourishment? How long would the beauty of the petals survive if not for the protection of the thorns?

Enlightenment Now

As I sat in the great meditation hall in South Fallsburg, I would watch the incredible spectacle that is darshan, or the time when everyone has the opportunity to greet the Guru and receive a blessing. This is truly a wonderful show unfolding in the spotlight of Creation. A Guru sitting in front of hundreds of people, laughing and gossiping with friends; throngs of people, awaiting their sacred moment to be anointed by the touch of peacock feathers on their heads. A Guru haphazardly waving a wand of feathers in front of her, all the while talking, pointing and laughing; swatting people who are in near ecstasy at being within a few feet of a recognized, enlightened being, anticipating the reception of her highest blessing.

It never failed to strike me how this scene played out, differently through each person's perspective, as we all shared in playing our part in the event. What might be life changing for one, would be a missed opportunity for another, and just another evening for yet another. At the same moment that a person could be feeling the thrill of God running through her veins, another person nearby could be wondering, "What's going on with her?" The thoughts we have been conditioned to choose to entertain can take us to heavenly heights, or hellish depths, and the mind has a moment by moment input in this choice.

Our inner worlds, the thoughts that color the way we see life, are our own creations, and few of us realize that this is really where we spend most of the time of our lives. We decide certain things are the attributes of an enlightened person, then we look for someone to fit our notions. Sometimes we search and finally decide, "No one exists these days who fits the bill, if only I had lived way back then, when saints roamed the earth." Or some of us find someone, listen to those around this person and begin to believe, "He's the one. He has what I want." Then we build up our picture of this person until what they have is something we could never attain. Either way, we are living in our inner fantasy, and either way we lose.

So if enlightenment is not the many fantasies our minds attach to it, what is it?

Enlightenment is an understanding that occurs in the mind. Nothing less, nothing more. When you understand how to tie your shoes, you are now a shoe tier. When you understand how to ride your bicycle, you are a bicycle rider. When you understand what the feeling of Self within really is, you are enlightened. It really is not any more complicated than that. You do not experience bells and whistles and lights flashing around you with this new understanding, but you do see yourself differently. Your mind has a better understanding of things as they are. Just as when you are a bike rider, you now understand your relationship with a bike in a different light, as an enlightened being, you understand your relationship with your inner Self in a different way.

Before you thought the feeling of Self was something your body and mind made. You thought that there was a Self that you had to get in touch with, a Self that was different from what you felt inside your body/mind. Your new understanding shows you that your old understanding was incorrect, that you have learned more and understand better. It shows that the feeling of me deep inside that you thought of as yourself was really always the feeling of Self that you were striving to know. You see that what you mistook for the personal was in reality all along the infinite. You stop identifying the small self that you thought you were with the mind and body, and start identifying it with the whole of infinity, the essence of all that is.

It really is a tiny little switch in understanding; a tiny switch that has profound implications. Once you switch the identification of the self to the Self, you understand that there was really never a person thinking otherwise. It was only a misunderstanding that said, "I am a person. I am a mother, a plumber, a cook, a baker…" The mind was the culprit here, misappropriating the feeling of Self as its own little self. When the mind sees its mistake, it can let go of its identification and allow the boundless Self to have its rightful place again. The feeling of Self can be felt in the body, but you also feel that it has no boundaries. It was the mind that limited the breadth of the Self to the body alone, but this limitation is only of the mind. There is one Self, one feeling of Self in the multiverse, and you are it.

Understanding this, accepting this and experiencing it is what it means to be enlightened. Understand this by reading these words and letting them connect to you current beliefs. Accept this by letting the old, incorrect beliefs be uprooted and replaced by this new understanding. Experience it by becoming silent and feeling the Self within and seeing that it really feels boundless, and is really all that you are.

Chapter Two: Who Am I?

Now that we have a better idea of what enlightenment is, an understanding that has been stripped of fantasy and unreal trappings, we can now better ask, "Who am I?" and "Who is this I that wants Enlightenment?"

Again, a good way to approach these questions would be to remove the fantasies that the world has created around who we are before truly identifying who we are. Whenever a concept has a lot of baggage, it is always best to get rid of what is useless before looking at the useful.

First of all we know we are not what we do. I am not a cook, a cleaner, a writer, a father. I am not a doctor, an engineer or a musician. None of the things I do, none of my relationships with things, activities or even people really define who I am. We use language in this way, "I am a …", but it isn't really a true statement.

Next we should see that I am not my body. This is the single biggest incorrect understanding humanity holds, and it is just wrong. We are not these bodies we find ourselves in. As the writer of the correspondence course once intimated, "These bodies are nothing more than spacesuits that allow us to live on this planet." We are not our spacesuits.

Most of us are very attached to our bodies, in one way or another. Either we like our body and appreciate its individuality, its little quirks and its loveable qualities, or we hate our body, complete with too many pounds, too much skin, and too many problems. It is either our friend or our enemy, and either way we wouldn't want to be without it. We say, "I am beautiful," or "I am fat," and take these descriptions to be indicative of how we are, not of how our body is. We identify with the body we find our life taking place in without a second thought.

If we were to lose all of our limbs, our senses, our torso, and be left as a heart and a brain, would we still feel a sense of me? Yes. Would we still be so attached to the body, what's left of it anyway, as we previously were? Probably not. We might begin seeing that the pieces of our body do not make us who we think we are. In fact there is no place in your entire body that you could say is really where you are. As long as the brain is able to function, you could remove piece after piece and never find a place that is exclusively where you are.

So are we the mind? Again, what part of the mind is you? Can you find a place in your mind without which you are not? Can you move this feeling of you in your mind from one place to another? Are you your memories, your thoughts?

Looking inside my mind, I can see the thoughts come and go and there is no I controlling them. I can see that I am not centralized in one location, but the feeling of I seems to be in the head, although that really is more a belief than something I can state with complete accuracy. During my experience of being the room, I felt I was each object in the room, so yes, in altered states you can definitely see the feeling of I is mobile. Memories and thoughts can be watched, but neither feels like me. Maybe there is an "I" that possesses all of these things, but there does not seem to be an "I" who *is* any of these things.

To understand this on a level that is deep enough to mean something to you, you must sit and look at where you find yourself. You must come to an understanding of what you are for yourself in order to move forward. If you believe you are your left big toe, you will be stuck there and realization will be far from you. If you do not go deep within yourself and examine whether you really believe you are your previous thought or your next, or if you are the awareness of them all and more, who will do it for you? If you do not understand this for yourself, and if you are not brave enough to discard identification with what you are not, then your Self can not shine forth from the background and will not be understood and experienced.

So if we can see and agree that we are not what we do, we are not the body we are using to do what we do or even the mind that knows all of what we are doing and thinking, then what is left? If we are not our role in this play of life, if we are not the costumes we wear or the lines we speak or the story we are enacting, what could we be?

When we eliminate all that we are not, we find that the only thing remaining in this play is the screen itself. The space that this play happens in is all that is left, and if we are nothing else, then we must be that. Why? Because we *are*, right. We feel that we exist, we feel that we have a beingness. This knowingness of existence is all we have, really and if it does not have any structure that we can touch, if it is not of a more ethereal quality as is mind, then we are left with being just a feeling in space, a mindless, bodiless feeling of I.

Could this feeling exist in another dimension, could it be the soul? If we are looking for something that is individual and personal, that has a connection to the person we think we are, then no. If you look at yourself at the deepest place you can feel, you see that all personhood melts away and there is nothing left but a *feeling* of being.

At our core we are all points of awareness in a sea of awareness, labeled as separate by the mind. The Soul that is synonymous with the Self which we all are, feel and share is the only one that you could really be. Pure, simple, complete, unattached, unfettered, and boundless I.

This is an examination you must carry out for yourself. Just as with a test, if I give you the answer, you won't really remember it in a day or two; if you don't examine this inner feeling of I for yourself, it will not mean anything to you. You may garner an intellectual understanding of these words, but you will not be any closer to the true dawning of complete understanding and the wisdom that can enlighten will be far from you. Experiencing this inner feeling of I is the first step towards truly knowing who you really are.

Seeing what we are not has led us to feeling what we are. How can we better get in touch with this inner space?

Meditation is the easiest way to take an inner journey and to have a visit with our Self. It is nothing more than sitting quietly with your Self. It allows us to let go of all the beliefs that we hold that make up our self and free the little self to become the real Self which we all share.

When you begin meditating, plan to set aside at least ten minutes to sit quietly and begin to know yourself. As you become more acquainted with your inner world, you can devote more time to enjoying it. Sit in a quiet place in a chair or comfortably on the floor with your back straight. Gently close your eyes. Turn your attention inside to an awareness of your inner space. Focus your moment by moment attention on the silent stillness within. If thoughts start to come up, when you notice they are there, bring your attention back to the space within. Allow your awareness to merge with the peaceful silence that is your Self within.

At times it is also helpful to use your breathing as a tool to diving deeper into your inner space. As you breathe naturally, become aware of each breath. Watch the breath as it comes in and as it goes out; just have an awareness of each breath. Feel the still point in between each breath, and feel the air as it enters your body and again as it exits your body.

Sometimes people find that if they can hold onto one thought, they can eventually allow the thought to float away and leave them in the stillness. They take a phrase or a mantra and repeat it over and over with each breath to focus the mind on one thing. You can repeat "I am" with each inhalation and "I am" with each exhalation. Feel the words in your mind, feel the space around each word before you say it to yourself, as you hear it inside your mind, and after it has finished. Feel the space that remains between repetitions of "I am." Know that words have a power of their own, and that the words "I am" vibrate at a frequency that is very helpful in meditation. Repeat this process over and over and allow it to carry you deeper inside. When you are comfortable, let the mantra cease and rest in the space you have recognized deep inside.

Many times during meditation when thoughts arise and continue, we tend to berate ourselves; "Why can't I just be quiet, why does my mind always have to chatter?" At this time we need to realize thought is the nature of the mind. Ancient sages did not consider it the "monkey mind" for no reason. Instead of trying to stop it from doing what it has done all of your life, a better strategy during meditation is to watch the thoughts. Become their witness and watch them as a person watches a cloud pass overhead. Do not become judgmental, do not become angry or attached to a thought and do not follow the train of thoughts. In fact, do not care about the thought at all, just watch it come and watch it go. With this little detachment you will find thought has no energy and instead you will find you have its energy which you can use to focus on your silent, inner Self.

After meditating for several days, you will begin to find that the feeling you encounter deep within every day starts to become very familiar. You see that it was there all along, and it was easy to overlook. The feeling of "me" within becomes easier to contact, easier to recognize and touch at will. It becomes something that you have an awareness of even when you are in the midst of other activities.

Now you can see that you are gaining insight into the answer to the question "Who is this I that wants enlightenment?" At this point, you can also understand that you are starting to see and feel the answer to the question, "Who am I?"

Chapter Three: What Do I Want?

When people think they know who they are, they then try to figure out what they want. All of us have gone through life with the belief that we want and need food, clothing, shelter, water, air, acceptance, love, contribution, success. The list goes on and on and gets more ethereal once we have the basics the body needs to survive.

We do the many things we do in life to attain these basics. We work, live and love to fulfill these needs. We play and compete and laugh in order to feel good, to believe we are worthy and better than others, to feel we are experiencing life to its fullest. We strive to get more stuff to feel happy.

What very few of us realize is that everything we want to do, all the activities that we participate in that make us happy, and all of the life experiences we seek have, at their core, the feeling of the Self. When we thought we were running for the joy of it, or competing to prove our skills, or watching that comedian to laugh, we really were answering, on a very deep level, the call of the Self within. As much as we thought we were chasing good feelings and fun, we really were chasing the feeling of the Self in all of the activities we immersed ourselves in.

We participate in sports, music or acting to feel the rush of the Self within. We experience it as being in the zone, or as losing ourselves to our actions and not thinking, only reacting. We ski to feel the Self; we take walks in the evening to know the Self. We eat good food, drink good wine, keep good company, seek the perfect lover and make good love to have a fleeting experience of the wholeness within, when the mind is at peace and the feeling of Being, the sense of the Self within can shine forth unfettered by the thoughts of an over-active mind.

There is not an action that any human performs that does not have at its goal experiencing the joy of the Self within, although with many actions this ultimate goal is hidden by intermediary landings. We want happiness which leads directly to the peace of the Self. We want respect, this leads to the stillness of the mind which leads to the experience of the Self. We want security which leads to stillness of mind which leads to the Self. We want love which leads to peace of mind and happiness which both lead to the Self. The path can be longer and more circuitous, but in every extensive analysis, one or another aspect of the peaceful, silent, blissful Self is waiting at the end of every path.

Armed with an understanding of who we are and an experience from meditation that shows us that we are not the body, nor the mind, but at our core we are a silent, vibrant space of Being, we can better understand what the real Self we all share wants.

We can quickly see that most of what we strive for on a daily basis are things that satisfy the needs and wants of the body and the mind. The true needs of the Self within are none of the things we mention as needs in life. The Self, the feeling of Being that lives within all of us, the same Self that you have touched during meditation and are beginning to understand as the true "me" doesn't have a mind or a body, so the things that our mind and body need do not apply to what we really are. In fact there isn't a thing in this material world, nor is there a concept, that this feeling of Being needs or wants.

Quite honestly it isn't even looking for enlightenment. Enlightenment is another concept for the mind to seek; it has not been requested and is not required of the Self. The screen of the play of life is receptive to all the play, but it needs none of it. It is an awareness of its own beingness, and it has not another care in all of existence. What we all are at our core is carefree and lightness beyond all thought. It does not have a mind to think, but all of this Creation rests on and in it.

It has been said from ancient times that the play of existence came into being for its own sake, and the totality of its purpose is only to play. The Beingness that we are is the foundation for all of Creation, all the Universe. The total cause is "I", the feeling of Being.

With "I am" comes the sea of Awareness in which each point can experience itself in relation to the whole and on which all of what we know of today as possibly a Holographic Multiverse including an infinity of dimensions, states, and vibrational possibilities comes into existence.

It is amazing enough to experience our Self in and out of meditation. It is absolutely incredible to begin to understand that this feeling of Self we all are at the core literally wants nothing, and needs nothing, and in fact does not even have the capacity to want or need or think. The Self is beyond all concepts the mind could entertain. And then on top of all of this the same Self that we are is the basis for all that we see and know in our lives. This is a little different from what most of us have always thought life to be.

Am I saying that basically the Self we all want to know, this feeling that we all crave in the things we do every day is nothing but a disembodied, thoughtless feeling of "I" that by the mere fact of its being creates all of Creation?

Well, yes, to the mind, it appears as such. But we have to understand the nature of the mind. Mind is a great tool to understanding a certain level of living. It can take vibrational input and convert it into a picture that makes sense. It can classify things and categorize objects and ideas and make this vibrational soup we actually live in seem ordered. It is also great at helping to delete the parts of this Creation that do not neatly fit inside the picture it has drawn. If a frequency does not fit into the narrative the mind has created for the person it has created or believes itself to be, then it will not transmit its existence. We discard much more than we receive every moment of our lives. The mind is also a good steward for the senses, but the senses themselves are very limited and are ordered to show a very small portion of the world. We will pursue this in much more depth shortly.

Chapter Four: So How Do I Get Enlightened?

Once we understand that neither the I who asks the question "How do I get enlightened?" nor the I who is a seeker of truth is the ultimate I who we all are at our essence, the question can be better understood. The I who we all are, wants and needs nothing, but the illusory I found in the mind/body identification wants a lot of what it believes it is not, and it feels an interminable need to continually add to itself.

Maybe the better question to ask before "How do I get enlightened," is "Do I really want to be enlightened?" If you understand that enlightenment isn't about all the glorious trappings that the mind would like to believe it is, is it really that desirable? Yes, you know your Self, but you also lose the person who you have thought you were for your entire life. Yes, your seeking will come to an end, but no, most people around you will still be seekers. You will know you share the Self of all with all, but you will more than likely be pretty alone in knowing this. Most of your friends won't have this understanding; probably none of your co-workers or neighbors will have a clue about this. Certainly most of your Facebook "friends" or Twitter "followers" won't be interested, know about, or even care about your new understanding.

So why go forward? If you are not going to have magical powers and know the universe, why bother?

Because the inner urge to know the Self, the inner calling is just too strong. We can turn it off for a day, a week, maybe even a few months, or more accurately we can stop listening to it for a time, but in the end, it is there in every activity we perform. When we laugh, we feel the Self; when we feel love, we feel the Self. It is the basis of all feelings, and it is the underlying reason we do anything that we ever do. When we don't know this, outer things have a pull that we do not understand; when we know this truth, outer things pull us with strings attached back to the Self which we can begin to observe.

Ultimately the honest truth is you really don't have a choice. Just as there is no you, which you come to understand on the other side of enlightenment, there is also no you to decide to become enlightened or to not continue on the path. When this Creation, which you as the Self permeate, sustain and enable decides something, who is there to decide differently?

As Being, you are the background or substratum of all Creation. The Universe is the play that happens on the screen that you are. You, the Self of all, have no say in what happens on the screen that you are. As the total and complete

Unmanifest Being, you do not know or care what is happening on the screen. You do not even know there is a play happening and using you as a screen. It does not touch you as you are so far beyond it and free from it to not even know it exists. The play just occurs, and Awareness, which is the closest thing to an interface between the Self and the world that exists, just watches. Awareness in its purest essence, at its stillest point is the Self; Awareness in the world is what we experience as the center of our consciousness. Awareness at the end of the spectrum that is the Self is aware of Being alone; Awareness more veiled at the opposite end of the spectrum that is in the world sees the movement and the differences which make up our daily lives. The mind adds names and further thoughts of differentiation, as a part of this immense universal play of Creation.

Creation, the total collective of the entire Holograph that is the Multiverse, creates itself continually, plays all parts simultaneously, and enjoys each point at each moment in the sea of Awareness.

"But I wanted 2 creams in my coffee," I say, exasperated that the waiter has already put too much milk in my cup. "The Universe must be conspiring against me," I think to myself. In reality all of the Universe has indeed conspired to create this exact moment, everything from wars thousands of years ago to decisions hundreds of years ago to explosions billions of years ago, all occurring so the Creation that is your body/mind, your here/now could complain about the coffee right now. That was the part it wanted to play in that moment, and it did it real well.

What if we could approach all actions we perform with that understanding, seeing that the whole of Creation is making each moment happen just as it has designed? What if we could complain less and appreciate more? Again, it would be part of the play if we found ourselves doing this. We would find the urge to do so, and the act of appreciating would be there. The act of our full participation is all part of the play, so we play the role as best we can. Before understanding life in this detail, we did what we did as part of the play; after understanding life and our place in it in its minutiae, we watch and witness what we do as part of the play. Nothing changes but the understanding in the mind and the acceptance that Creation feels.

When Creation decides at any moment that it is time for another bubble to burst, much like the water on the surface of the ocean, a bubble will pop and understanding will roll in, bursting the illusion of separation. Much like these bubbles, we always thought we were separate from the ocean, but with the bursting that enlightens each bubble, at the exact moment that the oceans decides it will happen, with the exact pressures which all the ocean bestows upon an individual point on its surface, the bubble melds into the whole of the ocean with the understanding that it is the ocean being experienced at a particular point in time. It is both the entirety and the point, simultaneously, just as we are the beingness we feel at the point of our body/mind as well as the entire Being that is behind the fullness of all Creation.

All of this is not to say that we are not part of this Creation, as we can see that Creation is the manifest aspect of the Unmanifest Being that we are. The essence of our feeling of the Self is Being; the actualization of doing, of our motion in this play is the Universal Creation. We feel our Self in our bodies as our essence; we see our works as this grand Holographic Multiverse.

So when we decide to understand that we are one with the Self of all, that what we feel as "me" inside of ourselves is the exact same thing as the universal Self, we have decided to be enlightened.

Although this is the final step and takes exactly a moment, most seekers are unable to accept that the tremendous goal they have aggrandized in their minds can be experienced this simply, so their minds instead need to undertake various practices which gradually allow the mind to accept this simple truth. If I had heard this truth so simply put at the start of my search, I doubt I would have been ripe enough to understand and accept it. Thus I began my journey walking what I could believe and accept as a path toward enlightenment.

When most of us first become aware of the concept of Self and enlightenment, few of us quickly reach a point of feeling we deserve the fruits right away. We need priming, we need to put in hard work, in order to believe we are worthy of the fruits. Once we have struggled and suffered and learned and failed and dusted ourselves off and tried again, cried again, and pushed through, *then* we believe we are ready to take that step over the threshold to the other side.

It took me three years of doing various practices that I felt best suited me. I was fortunate to have many from which to choose. My priming was faster than some, slower than others, but through walking these paths, I learned the keys.

Here is the story of my journey to realization.

Chapter Five: Awakening

I usually had meditation sessions where I would sit cross legged in a quiet space, get real still, close my eyes and watch my breathing. When my mind started chattering, I would repeat "I am" with each breath. During my time sitting I would see dull colors radiating in my inner eye behind my eyelids. Once in a while I would see a bright light and I would open my eyes to see what it was, but would find nothing unusual. Very infrequently my thoughts would have enough space in between that I could enjoy thought-free moments.

One Wednesday evening I was sitting on my bed in the basement of my parents' house meditating and after an hour or so of sitting I stretched my legs in front of my body and continued to meditate. I could hear my heartbeat and I took the sound inside of me. I heard an airplane in the distance, and felt my awareness expand to take the sound of the airplane within as well. I imagined my awareness going up 30,000 feet high to surround the sound coming from the engines of the plane.

I flew with the sound, feeling that it was coming from inside of me, not from something far away from my body. As I listened to the roar inside of me, all thought stopped. I listened as the sound became fainter and was shocked by the sound of the furnace cutting on outside of my room. In that exact moment I felt the sound of the furnace was inside of me too and I found myself expanding to become the entire room. Whereas before my awareness was of my body, now my awareness was of the whole room. I was the air in the room, I was the walls, the bed, the sliding closet door, the dresser; everything in the room was me. I intimately experienced my awareness in everything and then a thought arose. Very clear and surrounded by light, each word blazed momentarily in my head. "Wow, this is great! How could I ever have believed myself to be this tiny body?" I had the distinct impression that I was experiencing something I already knew, and I felt truly awake for the first time in my life! I was finally seeing things as they really were!

I sat in my expanded awareness for an indeterminate time, then saw another thought arise. "I wonder if this is my new way of seeing life." I sat still again and enjoyed the expansion. Awhile later another thought arose, "I wonder how long this will last," and another "I wonder how I can live like this," and another "Is this like a bubble around me, and will it be the same when I leave…"Then suddenly I felt a contracting and almost heard the sound "Zoom" as I found my awareness shrink back into my body.

I opened my eyes and looked around the room. I was ecstatic and had a huge smile on my face. I finally had a truly incredible meditation experience! I had awakened for the first time in my life! It was very clear to me in that moment that my preoccupation with my mind, specifically my love of my thoughts had kept me ignorant of my true being, and that I would never ever be the same again.

I laid down in my bed and went to sleep and the next day I awoke with a smile. Yes, I remembered it, no I was not dreaming, yes, what the great teachers say is true! We are more than our bodies and now I know it too!

I got up, put on my old jeans and tee shirt and drove to work, all the while expanding my consciousness. I opened the sunroof of my Jetta and felt myself expanding to the clouds and beyond. Although not as real as the meditation experience of the night before, the feeling was much more than just fantasizing. I had a real understanding that I was one with everything that I saw. I watched the air in front of me, I saw the car auras trailing behind the cars passing at a red light. I knew I was not just this little body anymore and could never see myself as just this person any longer. Life for me had changed completely, and could never be as it was before.

The entire day was spent feeling a truer perspective of being. I did not see from my eyes alone, I was not limited to seeing life from the vantage point of a person in a body. Instead I saw life as a witness of what this particular body was experiencing. It was as if I was physically stationed a couple of feet above and behind my body, so I was aware of not being the body, and also of seeing everything that it did as separate from me. This perspective also allowed me to take a longer view of my surroundings, to be a part of them much more so.

I was not just located in and surrounded by the thoughts in my mind any longer. The mental noise did not attract me as much anymore. Instead I was able to experience the life that was around me, the living that happened everyday while I had been paying attention to the thoughts, believing them to be more interesting and important than actually living.

It was an amazing feeling to be living instead of thinking about the life I had led, or the one I would be living, or the way I should approach what I might find myself doing at some future time. For the first time, I was not just going through the motions, thinking my way through life, but I was actually living and being aware of life as it happened.

It was truly liberating to begin to live life!

Chapter Six: Starting on a Path

By the end of the day my connection with my experience had decreased, but the memory was still vibrant, and I was anxiously awaiting my next meditation session. "What would this evening's meditation bring?" I wondered. "Would it validate my experience, or was what I felt a once in a lifetime experience?" As one o'clock in the morning came and I began meditating, I found questions swirling around in my head. "How had that happened last night? Will it happen again tonight? What can I do to make the experience come again?" I sat and watched the thoughts as best I could and slowly, gradually they subsided.

After sitting for over an hour, I found myself in the space of no thoughts once again. After an unknown time, I found myself feeling expanded again, without clear boundaries. The furnace again clicked on and I was triggered into being my surroundings. Once again, I was wide awake, in meditation! No thoughts, just feeling that I was everything. The same experience, a different night!

After an indeterminate time of basking in the amazing bliss of the thought-free state, being one with all around me, I again became more interested in my thoughts than the space of stillness would allow. My awareness was again sucked into my body and I lay down and went to sleep. Again I was ecstatic! I knew that I was more than I ever dreamed, and I could connect to that space whenever I wanted! I really was awake!

The night after that, Friday night, an old friend came to town, and I took her out, so I didn't meditate when I returned home after two in the morning. The same was true with Saturday night, so I didn't meditate again until Sunday night. I knew where the space of expansion was though, so I had no concern about being able to return these. I sat in deep stillness and watched my thoughts going around in my head, watched the shapes swirling in my closed eyes field of vision, heard my throat clicking, which I always thought was a sign of yogic chakra cleansing in deep meditation. I imagined myself expanding up into the sky, I waited and finally heard the furnace click and... nothing.

After sitting for two hours, I laid down, disappointed, but still in the afterglow of the two experiences of a few days earlier. I meditated most days the next week and the utter stillness of the thought-free state did not come to linger with me. There were no more experiences of expanding and being the room.

As a child of 12, I read a book, *The Transcendental Meditation™ TM® Book,* which my mother had. It was very cartoony and it seemed very much geared toward a child, so I followed the steps it taught and learned to meditate. I read books on ESP and felt the feeling of me within. At that time was living in Las Vegas and had just finished the sixth grade. I remember standing and closing my eyes and feeling my Self within and really communing with the feeling. Finally I said, "Remember this feeling. This is what I feel like as a 12 year old." As real as any other memory, I cataloged it and referenced it from that point as I grew older.

I can honestly say from that day to this, the feeling that I told myself to remember, that taste of my inner Self, was no different back then than it is today. Only the understanding of what that feeling was has changed.

To give these experiences a little perspective, here is a little about why I began meditating. At 13, I read a book my grandmother had when I was vacationing with her and my father in New Jersey. I spent the summer experimenting with *Instant ESP* with my father and sister, trying to see if we could manifest an experience of ESP. We would sit near one another and try to see if one of us could send and another receive the suits and numbers of a deck of cards. I tried to look at my aura between my fingers, and follow the other instructions in the book to touch an untapped power within.

By 15, I was reading *Silva Mind Control*, another book my mother owned, and trying the exercises within, still attempting to have a concrete, undeniable, and repeatable experience of ESP, or one of the other wondrous things this book promised.

As an 18 year old freshman at MIT, intent on becoming an astronaut and exploring the outer reaches of space, my stepfather gave me *The Science of Mind*, and I delved deep within to again try and experience the power that lies within. I reflected on something a Noble-Prize winning physics professor said to his recitation class one day, that as far as science had come, it could only answer the "How does this work" questions, not the "Why does this exist" ones. Science was not going to solve the age old questions of "Who am I," and "Why am I here?" When I heard these words, they were disappointing, and during my freshman year I found them hard to believe since there were so many equations that so accurately described the world.

By my senior year I learned that mankind didn't know all of what we claimed to as I watched a man who I admired, Ronald McNair, an astronaut I had the good fortune of meeting and speaking with only a couple of months earlier explode in the shuttle disaster of '86.

At this time I was 21. I took a year off from school to re-examine my direction and flirted with the idea of becoming a minister. I spoke with a minister who told me that I needed to have a love for the bible as this would be the book I would be living my life by and teaching from every day. I went on a Unity retreat with Eric Butterworth and had many great meditation experiences. One woman at the retreat came to me in an excited state at one point in the midst of the retreat to inform me that she didn't understand it, but from where she stood watching, it seemed as if I disappeared while I was meditating under a tree.

I spent the year living with my father in New Jersey, going out dancing Saturday night, then straight to church with him at the Lincoln Center in Manhattan on Sunday mornings. I became a Real Estate agent because he made it very clear that I could meditate all I wanted, but I had to support myself while living under his roof.

By day I would walk to work, stop at the park in South Orange and meditate. I would watch the clouds and envision myself seeing inside of them from above them, and watching my spirit soar. I would meditate while listening to soothing jazz by the Pat Metheny Group or Lyle Mays, and have joyful visions of being part of the dance of the universe. During one evening meditation I had a vision of a being in red being with me. At other times I had dreams or visions with Jesus or other religious figures.

When I returned to MIT, I had learned enough to understand that uncertainty existed in what was being taught, although I was unaware that a huge shift was taking place in physics with quarks and other sub atomic particles along with their amazing behavior beginning to take center stage. I did know that the answers I was seeking were not going to be found outside of myself, but were lying in wait deep within.

By the time I finished with my degree in Aerospace Engineering, I had a passion for seeking the truth within. I took a job with my mother and step father working in their machine shop in Atlanta. This allowed me to meditate into the early morning, read as much as I wanted, and delve into my inner world. I studied *Autobiography of a Yogi* by Yogananda, many books on various types of yoga, *Creative Visualization, The Tibetian Book of the Dead,* and *The Gnostic Gospels,* as well as several books on the philosophies of C. Castenada, J. Krishnamurti and P.D. Ouspensky.

A year into my studies I found myself reading a book on the role of meditation in various religions, *The Meditative Mind*, which a friend had sent me along with *A Spiritual Journey*. I was really immersed in meditation, sitting between one and three each morning to meditate most nights. In between I would go out dancing to meditate with the music.

I had read about enlightenment and wanted it. I had read about amazing meditation experiences and yearned desperately to experience them. After searching for this truth within for over 13 years, at 25 I felt ready to have a glimpse of reality. I had read all about it for so long, and if it was real, it was time for me to experience it. I truly had the deepest book knowledge on the ice cream of the soul; now I wanted to taste it!

After my most amazing meditation experiences of my life, I wanted to know more about them, I needed to know if others had similar experiences, but I did not have a clue about who to ask. I really felt the intense need to understand what had happened to me, and wanted to know what I needed to do to connect with it again. Finally I decided there had to be a book that could help me, so I went to a spiritual book store.

As I browsed the shelves, one title caught my eye, *I Have Become Alive*. I picked it up and by page 9 I knew this was the book for me. I picked up another book, *Play of Consciousness*, by the same author, Swami Muktananda, and went to pay for them both.

As I handed the cashier the money, she said that I picked two good books, and told me that if I was interested, there was a meditation center in town that was connected with this Guru.

"We listen to talks, meditate and chant," she said. "On Saturday nights, it's mainly chanting."

I had never chanted before, and had no real positive thoughts about the practice, but with my new perspective on who I was and what my life was, I was open to new things.

That evening, I went to the center and found a little slice of India in downtown Atlanta. The smell of incense and the sound of a tamboura greeted me as I walked in, and after a short orientation I walked into a room containing about 30 people. After an introduction by the emcee, the program began and I was chanting. It wasn't bad.

An hour later, I actually felt it was kind of good and enjoyable. We meditated right afterwards, for about ten minutes, and my only complaint was that we did not meditate longer. The chanting really set up a nice still space in my mind, but the meditation time was not long enough to dive deep within. I left that night with the feeling that I would definitely have to do this again.

In the next few months, I became a regular at the center, chanting and meditating on Wednesdays and Saturdays. The chanting really did help to focus the mind on one set of sounds, and make meditation come more easily. The meditations were never long enough, but the atmosphere was not one that I felt I could duplicate at home, complete with all the fellow meditators, so I enjoyed it as much as I could.

There was a special meditation program coming up on Labor Day weekend in upstate New York at the ashram, and shaktipat, the divine initiation was being given by the Guru herself, so I paid my money and made plans to drive up there for the program.

As the time of my departure approached, I was very excited. I was going to be given spiritual energy that would awaken my kundalini energy and help to move the spiritual energy up through my chakras and lead me to spiritual enlightenment. I had read about people being able to meet a Guru and have spiritual awakenings, but it had always seemed so far away to me, but now I was days away from having it happen to me.

On the drive up, I listened to chanting tapes, and by the time I reach South Fallsburg, I felt totally ready to meet the Guru and receive the spiritual awakening.

If I thought the center in Atlanta was a slice of India down south, the ashram in the Catskills was a whole Indian town carved into the mountains of New York. I checked in and walked to where the program was being held. I was disappointed to find the program was so full -thousands of people were there- that I was relegated to sitting in a hallway outside of the main meditation room. The sound was piped in so those of us in the hallway could hear the talks. I had a little square 3' x 3' taped off on the carpet which I could call my own, and that was where I was to spend the time for much of the program. I watched the people going into the main hall with envy, but I had not paid my money to take the program fast enough, so I had not earned a prime seat.

The evening session was the one everyone was looking forward to as that was when we would all be in an outdoor pavilion and most importantly, that was when the Guru would bestow the spiritual awakening upon us all.

I enjoyed the talks of the day, the celebrities sharing experiences, the scholars telling us about what these experiences meant, and the chanting. The meditations were nice and long, finally of the length I had been yearning for, but my little 3' x 3' space was cramped. Since it was a sign of disrespect to stretch your legs out in the presence of the Guru, even in the hallway I had to keep scrunched up.

When the night came, I followed the crowd to a beautiful glass building with a big ornate chair at the bottom where the stage area was located. My hallway status for the day allowed me access to one of the closer rows in the pavilion for the evening session. I had to have been no more than 15 rows from the big chair, and I took my seat on the marble floor and waited anxiously for the Guru's arrival.

When she entered the building, a hush fell on the crowd. She walked to her chair and sat, and we listened attentively to the speakers, all the while watching this enlightened being as she swayed in her seat. I looked around and could see people around me who could only be described as being in bliss. These people truly loved this woman, and they let their love show on their faces without any shame or fear.

The Guru spoke, and I enjoyed the talk. I had been hearing about shaktipat all day, what it would do to some people, how you could feel the energy running through your body, how it might make you shake or make strange noise, and I was happy to know that this transmission of spiritual energy would be unmistakable, and that I would have no doubt whether it occurred. The speakers had assured us that the few who would not feel anything would still get it, as it was guaranteed to be given to all who were part of the program, so I was satisfied.

The time finally came, and the lights were lowered and the Guru guided us into meditation. As we meditated she got up from her chair and walked through each row of meditators hitting everyone on the head or shoulders with a wand of peacock feathers. I tried not to be obvious in watching her, but as she came near me, I felt very excited and could smell the perfume on the feathers. A few people around me were making noises, so I was ready to feel this rush, then she brushed me on the head with the feathers and I felt… nothing. She hit me again as she walked on to the next person and with my eyes closed and trying to be in a meditative state I felt no difference from my normal meditations. As she walked away, I hoped she could know at some mystical level that she had somehow missed me, and would return to bestow my spiritual awakening upon me. As

I heard her get further away my hope shrank, and I knew I was one of the few who would not have a grand experience of awakening, but who would instead need to take it on faith that they had been awakened.

The next two days passed with more talks, more meditations, more chanting. It was nice, but I had really hoped to be one of the people who had felt at least a little jolt of spiritual energy. I didn't need a large dose, I would have been happy to feel just a tiny shock; static electricity would have been good, but I felt nothing.

It was also nice being in the presence of the Guru. She had an aura that made those around her feel peaceful and happy, and it was nice being around that energy, but there was no repeat amazing spiritual awakening for me during that visit to South Fallsburg.

Chapter Seven: The Practices

On returning to Atlanta, numerous devotees at the center informed me that even if I did not feel a thing, it was guaranteed that my spiritual energy had been awakened; what I needed to do now was delve into the practices. I decided to believe them and follow their instructions.

Initially I had been an avid meditator and that was my primary practice for many years. To this I had recently added chanting. Over the course of the next year I became a musician at the center, playing the cymbals and learning the drums and tamboura. I also started doing seva, or selfless service to the Guru. I did this by volunteering to do things around the center: cleaning, ushering during programs, sharing personal experiences during programs, and becoming a Master of Ceremonies for programs. I also found the practice of contemplation was well-suited to the way my mind worked, so I read everything I could find by Swami Muktananda and the other

Gurus of the lineage. Finally I delved into the bhakti or the devotional aspect of yoga and bought pictures of all the Gurus and attended as many programs with the living Guru via satellite as I could.

During this time, I continued to enjoy the chanting, and I found myself becoming busier with the other practices. I didn't meditate as much as I used to, but I was seeking the feeling of Self in all the practices I was doing. When I chanted, I would be cognizant of the feeling of Self deep within, and as I played cymbals I was aware that as I let go of my thinking self, I could play much faster than I had ever imagined possibly. I found myself entering "the zone" towards the end of an ecstatic chant, feeling almost as if the Self were taking over and I was left in a blissful spot, watching and enjoying the chorus of voices and the play of sounds all around me.

When I would immerse myself in feeling love for the Guru, again I could experience the feeling of the Self come welling up from within and take over my conscious awareness. During one particular program the Guru spoke of immersion into the form of the Guru, and I tried this and found that I too could feel the Guru, or the inner Self of the Guru within me. We took a nature walk during one two-day program, and I started noticing blue dots in my field of vision. I remembered that Muktananda had spoken of seeing the "blue pearl" in meditation, and I wondered if this was what I was seeing.

When we returned to the meditation hall, the program took a break, and I stood in front of a large picture of Nityananda, the Guru's Guru's Guru, feeling appreciation and devotion. As the feeling grew, I saw a blue dot appear on his belly. It stayed for a few seconds, then disappeared. I then saw another near his head, then another on his chest and before I knew it there were blue dots appearing and disappearing all over the picture. At one time there were over a dozen floating on his picture in my view. It was amazing, and I felt it was a gift from the Guru to see this auspicious sign of spiritual growth and connection with the Guru.

As I did more mundane practices like cleaning the shades in the center on a Sunday afternoon, I tried to envision that I was cleaning the Guru's ashram, or that I was participating in a great service to God. At first it was a game in my mind, but then there were moments when I could actually feel the Self within as I would work, and my attention to my thoughts would decrease.

Contemplating all of these practices, I could see that they were all designed to bring a devotee to an experience of their own inner Self. Whether it be from chanting, or meditation, or any of the other practices, the goal was the same: experiencing the Self within. After the experience with Nityananda's picture, I began to see that the feeling of the Guru within was one and the same as the feeling of the Self within. A devotee's part in this grand play is to put the object of their devotion on a pedestal, and in my doing this, I found that the inner strength, peace and stillness that I projected the Guru as having, were nothing different or less than what I was experiencing as my Self, within.

The next summer I drove my girlfriend to the ashram so that she could spend some time there, but I did not stay long myself as I really felt I did not need to be in the presence of the outer Guru, because I had installed the inner Guru in my temple within, and had recognized her as my own inner Self.

I continued doing the practices, and became one of the leaders of the center during the next year. I got even busier with all sevas that the leaders had to take care of, and continued to take as many courses as I could.

Another course I took was with one of the Guru's sevites, or workers who was in charge of a correspondence course. I enjoyed his talks during the course of the weekend, and by the middle of the second day, I found that random thoughts in my mind had stopped. If he was talking, I heard his words almost as if I were speaking them, not judging, but just hearing them. When he stopped talking, I stopped thinking.

It was an amazing feeling, a feeling of total freedom, and it felt very natural. As the program ended, I helped where I was needed, made sure all the arrangements were in order for the speaker to get to the airport, then I went home with a completely still mind.

I woke up the next morning and was still in this state. I went to work and had an entire workday with the clearest mind, the highest state of presence ever. Work was just loading steel on the automatic machining mill, watching it cutting, experiencing the action and sounds of the coolant splashing on the cutting surface and the steel chips being flung away, unloading the finished part, and loading the next piece of steel to repeat the process. No thinking, just experiencing the day. It was a blissful experience.

I was schedule to be the MC for the next program in a few days, so late in the afternoon I called my tutor, a sevite who would help make sure everything I said sounded good. For the first time in over a day, I found myself thinking beyond the act I was participating in. I watched my thoughts as I interacted with the tutor, then I listened to my inner conversation as I got angry about a statement she made that I took as a harsh criticism against my presentation. I found myself slipping away from the thought-free state and back to a place where my mind had thoughts, judgments, angers, likes and dislikes. I was back to what I considered my normal self.

Once again, I had had an amazing experience that had been cut short by my love for my thoughts.

After this, I began branching out and reading books from other disciplines, other spiritual teachings that might help me to better triangulate my understandings. I also decided it was time to spend some quality time in the Guru's presence. I went to South Fallsburg to spend a couple of weeks dedicated primarily to serving. Some people were able to leave their lives and live with the Guru permanently, but that was not what I saw as my path. It was tempting, and I felt the dedication, but for all my yearning for knowing my Self, I also believed I had the life of a householder, the life as a husband and father ahead of me, so I was happy to be able to put aside two weeks to spend immersed in the practices.

I was assigned the seva of hosting, so I got to open doors and direct people, to guide people as to where to put their shoes, to greet and welcome people as a representative of the Guru for the many programs being held during the summer. I got to stand guard near her quarters, and watch the hundreds who would sit waiting for her to pass. I got to seat people during programs and direct people to the line when the evening program was over and people went to get the Guru's blessing.

For me it was wonderful being a professional greeter, being allowed and actually being expected to be happy, pleasant and helpful to everyone all the time. It was as if the universe said, "This is the natural way everyone should behave with everyone else, so for two weeks, I am making it your job to be loving and pleasant to everyone!" Many people enjoyed peeling potatoes for meals, or gardening, but for me, this was perfect.

Towards the end of my stay, I was outside the meditation hall for one of the major courses, and I could hear the Guru speaking. I could not catch all of what was being said, but the essence of what she said shook me to the core. I realized why it was so important to be in the presence of the Guru. Some things could be written in books, some things could be put on video tape, but certain things had the most power when you heard them live. I heard her say that we all think we are people, but we are not. We are the Self.

So simple, yet too profound to really understand. Either you accept this, or you think it is crazy. I accepted it and this acceptance began to eat a hole in my concept of who and what I really was.

Back home, a book I dove into was "I Am That" by Nisargadatta. He said the same thing -that we are the Self- over and over. He also said that he was able to become realized, to know the Self in three years by trusting the words of his Guru. In essence he said, "I believed him, I trusted my Guru, and I felt the sense of my separation from the Self that the great Gurus know as their inner being melt away."

I began to clearly realize the key to all the practices. They were eventually about losing yourself, about letting go of the ego that thought it was so great, the ego that thought it was a person who does everything and whose perspective is always right. Each practice, in its own way for each type of ego and person, gently melts away any sense of separation- if you are lucky. If you are not, but if you still persevere, it will smash and crush and chop away everything you hold dear as yourself, until the Self stands is all that remains, standing there alone and lonely with no second.

One May afternoon as I read "The Mystique of Enlightenment," in the two bedroom apartment where my girlfriend and I lived, the final light went off in my head. If you have heard the story of the student of Zen who became liberated upon realizing the answer to a question his master posed in a talk, my moment was a clear as this. In the midst of reading U.G. Krishnamurti's words which in effect I understood as being, "Enlightenment is so built up in the minds of seekers, but in reality it is nothing but the way you are naturally. If you eliminate all the trappings that the mind expects, you are left with yourself, and that is The Self." He did not make it seem like some nearly unattainable goal, which I as a seeker had built it into, but instead made it clear that what we all seek, we already have, if we would just recognize it.

As this understanding hit home, all thought stopped, all seeking stopped, and at that moment, there was no I wanting anything anymore. What remained was just freedom!

Amazing freedom!

I knew who I was, what I was, and that there was no I who I was any longer. I knew the I that I felt was a universal feeling that we all share, and that we all are when we want to think of an "I". I knew the mistake that the mind makes, that the ego makes in confiscating this inner feeling and labeling it me. All the words I had read, all the seva I had done, all the chanting and meditation and contemplation and devotion all culminated into a single moment of knowing that went beyond all knowing, an acceptance of what I really was, and a relinquishing of all attempts to label the Self differently from what it really is.

I had recognized the key and let go of the need to be a person separate from the Self!

Later after basking in the truth of reality for a while, and laughing at the irony of the search which all seekers create – making a Self separate from you at your essence, then searching for it - I shared the experience with my girlfriend. What could she say, other than great? I knew she was happy for me, and that she wished she could experience it too. I also sensed that she only half believed it could happen like that,

since realization for most is an ideal that is always just a little out

of reach.

Can you ever tell someone, "Oh yeah, by the way, I'm

realized?"

Chapter Eight: Life after Enlightenment

As simple and subtle as the shift in understanding was for the person who I used to think of myself as being, from the outside looking in, life didn't appear to change much. I didn't leave my job and live on a mountain, I didn't become a famous spiritual celebrity, and I didn't get lots of strange powers or start seeing the future. Instead I continued to live my life as a part of the play of existence. I continued putting steel on a mill and watching it get machined, I continued going to the center and chanting and meditating and MC'ing. I even continued in my relationship, going up and down with the emotional play most relationships are.

From the outside there was no difference. The first lesson after realization taught by my girlfriend was that since there were no lights, no bright glow around my head or body that was easily recognizable, there was no way to share with others that realization was indeed attainable. So I shared my realization with no one else.

I saw the Zen quote was true as I went to my parent's house to help my step father chop wood to put away for the winter. I saw that before realization it was "I am this, I am that," and after realization it was "not this, not that." I was still in the play, but I knew that the real I was the background of the play. I participated, but I didn't lose my true Self anymore. I knew I was one with all, including the Guru, and the street sweeper and everyone else.

I also knew that enlightenment was never in all the experiences I coveted during my search. The experiences were nothing but part of the play. My perspective, or more accurately the perspective of this awareness and interpreted by this mind had shifted. Nothing else changed. Where before I saw a person living a life and seeking enlightenment, now there was a body with a mind that had the awareness of the Self within. Living happened, seeking stopped, the play of life continued.

As the years passed, I played my role well, shifting jobs when it was time to grow professionally, changing partners in love when it was time for further emotional growth, moving away from the center when it stopped fitting into my life.

Contemplation continued, as did meditation, but only because I enjoyed these activities, not because I was seeking something from them. Gurus would always say they continued the practices that led to realization because they enjoyed them, and now I found this to be true.

When I met the woman with whom I intended to spend my life start a family, I asked the woman who sold me two books many years earlier and introduced me to the center to officiate at my wedding, and chanted with her and other friends after the ceremony.

Since then I have had four children and lived a householder existence, complete with bringing our children into the world, paying bills, staying up late with sicknesses, struggling with the issues of marriage, jobs and life.

And yes, through it all, the perspective of the Self still lives. Sometimes it is stronger, sometimes nearly forgotten, always just a breath away from being as vitally present and vibrantly real as ever.

In the past few years, I have enjoyed reading contemporary writers like Eckhart Tolle, *Power of Now*, Leo Hartong, *Awakening to the Dream*, or Rupert Spira, *The Transparency of Things*. Nisargadatta's, *Prior to Consciousness*, edited by Jean Dunn continues to charm and show me new perspectives as well.

I write myself, as I have for many years, and I enjoy revisiting my own perspectives, which still are ever evolving. Just because the Self is known and experienced doesn't mean the mind stops trying to organize things in a variety of manners.

What it does mean is that there isn't a person here anymore to take credit for the organizing, and there isn't an ego there needing to be in control. There also is no attachment to a particular perspective, but just an understanding that appearances will change, understandings will evolve, and meaning is only for the mind.

It is only recently that this character in the play of life has decided to share writings with the world. After 22 years, it is time to share this particular perspective with the world. The reception of *How to Become Enlightened in 12 Days*, my first public writing on enlightenment has been nice.

In that book, I wanted to share the essence of my experience with enlightenment and to show that enlightenment is already yours, mine and everyone's, and it only takes a tiny shift in understanding to experiences this. I also wanted to share games the mind can play in order to show itself that what we each initially believe ourselves to be is a lot less than what we actually are. Finally I tried to let people have a place where they could return to short but deep exercises that would connect them with joy, peace and stillness within.

The feedback has been good, and I have heard from some who have shared this experience. I realized it was now time to give a fuller, more detailed explanation for those whose minds need to chew on more information before letting go and leaping into the freedom of liberation.

It was time to condense my many years of searching and experiencing into concise keys that could assist others in understanding what is true in their lives.

The primary practices or paths I found most beneficial that we will explore now in detail are: love and devotion, service, meditation, and the intellect. We will now walk these paths and gather the keys they have to offer.

Chapter Nine: The Path of Love and Devotion

The path that appeals to people who live mostly in their hearts is the path of the devotee or the bhakti. Many saints and realized beings are known in many religions to have attained the highest unity with God through one-pointed devotion and love towards the form of God for which they had an affinity. The Gopis in Hindu tales attained realization through their unerring devotion towards Krishna. Saints including Francis of Assisi, Margaret, and Saint Anthony all attained their highest unity with the same all-consuming devotion to their chosen form of God, Jesus. Sufis throughout history are known for their feverous dance of the dervish which is an expression of the extreme devotion and love they feel for their deity, which Rumi is known to have expressed through poetry.

We all can see this devotion in action when we observe a mother watching her young baby as she takes her first steps. We can see it when a lover laughs when spending precious moments with their beloved. We can see it in the eyes of a child as they play with their favorite toy.

We can also recognize one-pointed focus when we see a tennis player focusing on hitting the ball during an intense rally or a skier slaloming down a steep, slippery hill. We see this same intensity when a tightrope walker is in the middle of the high wire stunt, when musicians are playing deep inside a groove or when an actor has lost himself in a role.

When you are in love, you look at your loved one's picture all the time. You gaze lovingly into the eyes you see staring out of the picture. You miss their presence and wish you could be with them.

You can do the same with your spiritual practice of devotion. You take a picture or image of your loved one and enjoy it lovingly. Gazing at one who has attained the state you wish to attain helps to place that feeling of Self, which you can sense they are at one with, deep within your awareness. The Self is always with you, always *is* you, but in order to understand this, in order to experience it, we first recognize it in another, then transfer that feeling of the other into ourselves, then finally recognize that what we have turned into, which we at first thought was our beloved, is nothing other than what we were all along.

We also repeat our loved one's name, when we are in love. The repetition of a mantra, or japa, is the spiritual embodiment of this lover's way of basking in their loved one's glow. Repeating the name of your beloved, "Hare Rama", or that you love your inner divinity, "I love you, God" over and over brings the mind to focus on your loved one. Just as when you gaze at a picture of one who embodies the realization of the goal you seek, repeating their name creates a picture of them in your mind. Repeating their name focuses your energy within and allows you to again feel the space that your beloved lives in.

Chanting is one practice that allows us to feel devotion for our chosen divinity. When you chant you sit in an upright position on a chair or with your legs crossed and you repeat the words of the song, or chant. Chanting is a tremendous group activity, but can be done alone or with a recording of a chant. The words are usually various names or aspects of God, or devotional words. If you think "I love you ___," and fill in the blank with your chosen form of God, be it the Infinite, or Jesus, or Krishna, or the Self, or the Guru, or the Universe or something else. If you repeat this over and over for 30 minutes, you really begin to feel the one-pointed focus that the chant produces, and the love wells up within.

Practiced continuously, the person who has a strong connection to their heart center will begin to feel the heart open and the love pouring forth for the object of their devotion.

When the love becomes extremely high, the pain of separation is also felt. This pain is akin to the pain felt when a mother is forced to return to work after nursing a newborn for the first weeks of her life, or the pain new lovers feel when one must travel away for business. It is a longing to be with the other, and it is also felt as a need or a yearning to bring the loved one inside of oneself. Your love becomes so strong that you want to take shelter in your beloved, and you want your beloved to be sheltered in you. You feel the need to eliminate separation and for the two separate entities to merge into one. This is when love and devotion have reached their zenith. And this is when you can understand and experience the nature of the key that is devotion.

When you look outside and see your love any distance from you, you want to bring them near. With this yearning, over a period of time, you begin to feel that your love is with you, even when they are not. You begin to feel their ways, their being, their smile, their light within your body, and you begin to see that they really are not separate from you at all. This is when the two become one, when the beloved becomes the beloved, when your self merges with the Self.

When I practiced devotion with a picture of the Guru, I could feel their presence deep within. I felt the same energy I experienced in the Guru's presence when I looked at his picture. The Guru is a principle that is beyond a person, so I literally felt the same presence from a living body, and a picture of another body that had been dead for many decades. Repeating the name of the Guru or a form of God did the same for me. All japa became, "We Are One." The repetition of the mantra became so ingrained that it arose spontaneously during sleep. To this day it is the first thought that comes up when an emergency occurs, be it having a ton of steel drop on my foot, or delivering a child of mine. Whenever peace and focus are called for, the mantra is there for support and instant immersion in its goal, the stillness of the Self.

Whenever I chanted, usually in a Hindu name of a form of God, all chanting became "I Love God." "Hare Rama, Hare Krishna," became ecstatic because I could feel the love of God within with each word, honoring, praising, worshipping and becoming one with the object of worship.

Devotion derives its meaning from the devotee, and if you imbue it with the highest, most divine, loving and accessible joy you can fathom, its fruits will be yours to pick and enjoy.

Chapter Ten: The Path of Service

Service is another practice that resonates with certain types of people. Most of us like to think we are helpful to others, and some make it a large part of their lives to give of their time and energy to improve the lives of their fellow man. Others of us have jobs or do work that contributes to society one way or another. Either way, what we do can be seen as service, whether it be to a boss, to a company, or to a specific recipient of our actions.

When we perform work in a church or meditation center or other spiritual place, we are volunteering our time and serving what we can view as a mission of God. When we can see that our actions are serving God, then we are performing spiritual service or seva.

This is a practice that takes the mundane tasks we perform to keep our chosen place of worship and devotion active, and enlivens our work with a special purpose. Instead of just wiping tables after eating, we are doing a service to God, and we are giving back to God by offering our time and energy.

As we do this, we are usually performing a task that does not require a lot of thought, so we can become the witness of our body as it performs the task. As the witness, we see an act performed which previously might have been accompanied by a lot of mental noise. Before recognizing wiping a table as a spiritual act, the mind might have complained, "Why do I have to do this boring task, why me?" There may have been mental resistance to helping out or resentment that you were not more highly thought of and that your time is being wasted in menial tasks.

With a new understanding behind the task, your spiritual service instead becomes a joyful gift. Instead of resenting your motions, you can appreciate that they serve a useful purpose, and are a way of giving to the one you love. Much like when you give of your time and energy to a child or a lover, you feel happy to share the gift of your action with them; the same is true of giving in service to God. Your action becomes a reflection of your relationship with the world.

When the mind resists, an action is painfully performed, and when the mind is at peace, the same action produces much tastier fruit. Your experience of life is all about the reaction of the mind. When you give to a loved one, or when you give to God, the act of giving makes you feel closer to the one to whom you are giving. When you keep your mind on God or the Guru during service, you are focusing on the essence of the recipient of your actions. While serving, your one-pointed focus of your clear, peaceful mind lets you feel the peaceful place that the object of your giving experiences. You begin to feel the Self of the recipient welling up within, and you feel yourself, through your action, gradually and naturally becoming one with the object of your giving.

The act of giving generously of your time catapults you into sharing in the generous state of the object of your gift. You give to God and God gives back to you, and you are again becoming focused on God, and giving in love and devotion to the divine in your life.

Since very few of us can spend all of our time in service, unless we have given up a worldly life, we should allow service to permeate the non-worship related work we perform. While at work, if we can see that the ultimate recipient of our time and effort is still God, although there may be other intermediaries, like the boss, the company, and the shareholders, God finally receives the fruits of your work. Everything you do, in this sense, can be seen as spiritual service, and all actions you perform can be recognized as serving God, giving back to the Universe.

As you find yourself performing loving and giving actions dedicated to the Source, you find you feel in harmony with your actions, and you find your mind does not fuss about what you are doing. A peaceful mind and a cheerful demeanor allow you to recognize that every action really exists in tune with the Universe, that in fact action is performed because the whole of Creation has conspired for it to occur in the moment in which it does, and you are in accord with all of it. This leads you to feeling and appreciating the experience of the Self within, and you resonate as one with the goal of service. In the end, you find that you are serving the Self in all, and that you, the Self, are in reality serving your Self.

The alchemy of the practices shows that what you dedicate yourself to, without reservation, as the object of your devotion or service, turns you into the goal of your service, the Self. This key understanding runs through all practices, and as we develop the eye to see this, it becomes more apparent that the Self is using a myriad of ways to show us the same teaching, again and again.

The only difference is in the individuality of people, or the variety of life experiences we hold as who we are and where we come from. Each practice resonates with different people, and is used to bring them to the same goal. Whether you are standing on the east side of the mountain and must be told "Head west to reach the top", or you are on the south side and must receive the direction "Go north in order to scale to the pinnacle," the ultimate goal is the same, only the path you must take will differ.

Chapter Eleven: The Path of Meditation

The practice of meditation is a wonderful practice, and again certain types are drawn to its shores. When you meditate, you close out all the outer world, and dive deeply inside the ocean within. You become one with the stillness, silence and peace that meditation leads you to experience. Some would even say meditation does not lead to an experience of these things, but to the absence of outer experiences, which opens you to knowing what has always been within, only awaiting your attention.

A consistent meditation practice will begin with meditation every day at about the same time. Find a quiet, secluded spot in your home where you can put a mat or cushion, or comfortable chair. The early morning and late night are both good times for many as the demands of life are not as strong as at other times. Begin with meditating for ten minutes a day, and gradually let your time spent in your practice to increase. Use the instructions given in Chapter 6, and allow meditation to lead the way. You will find before too long you will be meditating for an hour each day, without a problem. When the body becomes trained to sit still for an extended amount of time, the mind can follow. Meditation time can increase beyond an hour to an hour and a half or even two hours a day, although for many of us, this is not practical with the many demands of life.

Instead, as you become a seasoned meditator, you will find that meditation can leave the meditation space. You find that when you arise from meditating, you do not leave the feeling of peace behind, but carry it with you to your first activity of the day, if done in the morning, or to your sleep if practiced in the evening. You find that activities performed during the day are full of the state of meditation. When you are waiting in line at the bank, you turn within and find meditation can happen, with your eyes open and your body standing! When you are eating, you see that meditation occurs when you focus all your attention on chewing and savoring the flavor and texture of the food as it passes into your body.

Soon you realize the same feeling of peace that you love in meditation exists in everything you can do during the day. The feeling of the peace of the Self, the calm you previously thought existed only for your hour a day, is hiding in all the numerous activities of your day. It was waiting for your mind to become quiet enough to recognize it. Where before you walked down the street thinking about what you needed to do or about what your friend thought of your clothes, or what that guy you met the other day is doing now, or a million other things, now you can walk down the street and just walk down the street. You can feel the street under your feet, feel the ground vibrating with each step. You can feel the breeze on your face, the air blowing your hair. You can feel the sun on your skin and hear the sounds of the day -the cars, the birds, the voices, all of it- and all of it full of the fruit and goal of meditation, a still peaceful mind that opens your awareness to you inner Self.

Meditation also opens your mind to other states, to amazing ideas, to a myriad of thoughts and possibilities, lights and sounds. It is as if the quiet mind does not want to be quiet, and will fight to be active by throwing things at you that will grab your attention. Many people have had their meditation practice sidetracked for years because they heard voices and started channeling them into this world. Others got so involved in the lights and shadows of other dimensions, and again lost themselves inside of their mysteries. Still others find a fantastic idea and stop meditating to pursue it.

It is very important to know what the goal of your meditation is and to remind yourself of it constantly. If your goal is to start a business, or to converse with beings from another realm, then do so, but if your goal is to know your true inner Being, then remember this and don't allow yourself to be distracted by the mind's play.

Just as you let thoughts flow past you without taking ownership, do the same for the visions the mind throws before you. Watch them, but don't be tempted. The greatest jewel the mind guards is the Self, but the mind will only give this treasure to the one who is persistent in asking for it. If you are daily distracted by something other than inner Peace, the mind will give you that other thing. Don't settle for less than you can have, and the energy of mind will dissolve into the Awareness that we are within.

The thought-free state is a space that opens you to many possibilities and many experiences, but again, stay focused on the goal that lies just beyond no thoughts. The inner feeling will in time open up and you will see its many wonderful aspects including Love, Joy, Peace, Bliss and Contentment. All of this belongs to the meditator who does not settle for less than the real goal of meditation.

When I started meditating, I was very keen on having my kundalini awakened. I had read that this was important for good meditation, so I figured I needed it. When I went to the Guru to get it, I was disappointed that it didn't seem to happen, as I thought it was all about a lot of bells and whistles. It took me many years to actually understand the spiritual energy, and I realized that my energy was flowing many years before meeting the Guru.

For someone who is new and ripe for an inner jolt, coming into contact with the frequency of the Guru can bring unusual sensations, but for me, my vibration was already at a level where I could meditate for hours. My kundalini was already wide awake. I understood that those who can sit for an extended period of time are already experiencing their energy body flowing well, with a kundalini that is energized and cleansing. The Guru, not being confined to a particular body, but being a universal principle will be there to guide your mediation and gradually awaken your energy. The fact that you can sit for meditation is enough to show that your kundalini is awake and cooperating and guiding you to experiencing its fruit.

Let your meditation practice give its gifts to you, and don't settle for flashy trinkets! With dedication, you will understand that meditation is handing you a golden key you have already seen, that of the experience of the Self within, an experience that is not confined to your sitting space twenty minutes a day.

Chapter Twelve: The Path of Contemplation

The next practice we will discuss here is what we have been doing all along: contemplation. My use of the term contemplation is not the classic, yogic contemplation, or samadhi, but instead the use of the mental capacity of the intellect as a tool for deeper understanding. While yogic contemplation is a stage between concentration and meditation, this contemplation is akin to the age old thorn used to remove another thorn, to be cast away once its work is done. Contemplation can occur when you read a useful book or when life shows you an intriguing connection. Anytime your life presents you with an experience which you recognize as being an integral part of your spiritual journey, the opportunity to go deeper into understanding it and yourself through contemplation awaits.

Contemplation is the practice that helps you see that all practices have pitfalls and distractions, and it is the practice that shows you all have commonalities. The goal that each practice is directed to is the same, although each practice approaches the mountaintop from a different angle. Contemplation takes each path and allows you to cull out the dross and keep the nectar. It assists you on each path to better discern your direction. It is the file that helps you clarify your keys.

On the path of devotion, contemplation becomes the voice that says, "My beloved is inside me." It is the voice that recognizes that the Self that you love in your chosen face of the divine is also inside of yourself and inside of everyone you meet. It ultimately shows you that this feeling you treasure so deeply after recognizing it as your beloved was always within you and others, only previously sitting unrecognized.

On the path of service, contemplation shows you your service is not restricted to your place of worship. It shows you that you can know the joy of serving the world the same way you can know the joy of serving your God. It also allows you to appreciate that the inner feeling of service is the Self, which you can recognize in all activities.

Without contemplation, the practices may bear fruit that goes unrecognized for a long time, but with contemplation, the seeker moves much faster to seeing the goal in all.

Contemplation is similar to meditation in that you sit quietly with your eyes closed and turn your attention within. It differs from meditation in that you are focusing your awareness on thought, and are considering one particular topic, the Self. You use contemplation to see the Self in everything. Like a shape hidden in a children's drawing game, the Self sits hidden inside all, just waiting to be seen, and contemplation is the magnifying glass that gives you the vision to see.

One day you may contemplate a passage you read in a book. You simply take the passage deep within and allow the mind to examine it from all aspects. As you have undoubtedly done in this book when passages pause for moments of contemplation.

Knowing that there exists a connection between all, contemplation can usually go deep enough to find the connection and bring back an understanding that is useful in your life. At other times you can contemplate a practice, or search for an inner teaching contained in something that happened in your day.

Armed with the belief and understanding that the Universe is working to bring you to understand your Self in many ways, both ways that you know and ways that you don't, you can see the hand of God pulling you ever closer in the activities of your day. Instead of "Why me," it is "I see how that is helping me to focus on what is real." With this higher understanding of motives behind occurrences, we do not approach life as a victim of the vagaries of existence, but instead see that we are being guided, sometimes gently and at other times forcibly to know what Creation wants us to know.

Contemplation can be like a snake on the trail of a mouse. It will smell it and search it out with vigor and cunning. At times you do not know where a train of thought will lead, then suddenly you are pouncing on the mouse and it all makes sense! Sometimes it may feel like a self-guided tour through your beliefs, but in the end, when you see the connections, you understand it was really only a Self-guided stroll to your goal. As with all practices, you should trust that the hand behind it, the one that is leading the way and opening the trail ahead, is the One you are seeking, deep within, the same One who has been calling you for much longer than you have known.

If you merge the practice of contemplation with you chosen path, you will easily understand and experience what your path is really about. Whereas before you may not have understood love, or you may live in your heart, and devotion was enough for you, when you contemplate the feeling, you let the mind deepen its understanding, building on your experience. The experience will then have a basis in understanding (mind) as well as in your feeling (heart).

Previously you might have enjoyed serving others, but now understand, with the help of you contemplation that what you were really always serving in others was the Self that shines brightly in all.

Before contemplation meditation was a thing you did every day; after contemplation, meditation becomes the next breath you take in each moment of your life.

Do not just take my word for it though. Examine the moments of your life, look into the practices you perform on your chosen paths and really begin to recognize the Self I them all. The Self is the only one playing hide and seek, and it is up to us to realize this key truth and see the Self camouflaged in the multitudes, awaiting our discerning eye and understanding mind to see it is all only me.

Chapter Thirteen: Summary of Other Paths

Other paths exist that are just as useful to various types of people. The ones we have discussed are the ones that I found most useful, but that definitely does not mean other paths are not viable and helpful.

Hatha yoga is great for people who are in tune with their bodies. It helps set the stage for experiencing the energy of the body. It also helps to put you in touch with your breath and your senses. It can also be a great way to get the body in shape for hours of sitting in meditation. In other words it sets a great foundation for the meditation practice. It can also be another distraction that leads many to believe the toned body that it leaves is its fruit when in reality this is a trinket for which many practitioners have settled for years.

As with all practices, when you begin, you need to keep your goal in mind. If you are doing it for exercise, fine. If you are performing a posture to experience your inner Self, then keep this goal in mind as you move through the asanas. Understand the one-pointed focus on your goal is at once a focus on the path as well, as with every step, the Self is inside of each footfall. In the end, the journey to the Self is made of a million steps, each on the Self, until we finally recognize the path on which we were walking.

When you are performing hatha yoga to know your Self, you are breathing in a manner that keeps you mindful of each breath. You are also moving your body into postures that help you awaken and move the inner energies of your more subtle energy bodies. With yoga you are becoming aware of the union of your body and mind and allowing that knowledge to take you within to the experience of the Self.

A good practice is repetition of the Salutation to the Sun. Repeating the twelve positions of the Sun Salutation with a high mindfulness of the movements of the body can take you deep within.

Usually after the vigorous motions of hatha yoga, the last part of a good session is resting while lying down on your back in savasana with your legs spread apart and your arms open and away from you. While many people do not avail themselves of the fruit of this posture as it is such a basic position, after performing yoga, complete with watching your breath, being aware of the motion of the body, and feeling the energy as you hold various poses, the mind and body have joined in moving together and in one-pointed focus on the present action. As you lie still, your mind will naturally follow your body and become still, taking you deep into a meditative state. Do this for 5 to 15 minutes and allow your mind to stay in its still place and feel your Self within.

This is much like the fruit of a good chant. The motion of the sounds combines with the one-pointed focus of the repetition of the chant, and when the chant is over, you are left with silence, which can take the mind to the still space that allows the Self to be experienced.

With enough practice, hatha yoga becomes an extension of the way you approach life. You become more aware of your body in all situations, and your movements become more graceful as you have a heightened connection between your body and mind. Your continual thoughts which were normally the background of your life are gradually replaced by mindfulness of your actions as you perform them. The stillness you train yourself to experience during the course of a yoga session eventually can begin to permeate the rest of your life, if you practice awareness during the poses.

If you contemplate what is happening here, you can observe that this is much like what you experience as the fruit of the practice of service, which similarly has as a large component the moving of the body and being aware of your thoughts as you perform your actions.

Another practice that has helped many people is the practice of mindful breathing or pranayama. When you sit and watch your breath, you are training yourself to breathe correctly in meditation. When you can take this practice into your daily life, you are using a natural tool the body provides to retain a piece of your attention as the witness of your body/mind.

In my early twenties, meditation gave me the gift of the energetic breath, which I still experience daily. With each of these breaths comes an amazing experience of the bliss of the energy body welling up within. It is said that this breath brings with it health and heightened senses, and it is my experience that it also brings peace and joy.

As you breathe in, you can feel the cool air entering your nostrils and filling your lungs. The more attention you can give to this process, the closer you can get to feeling your inner energy bodies. With each focused inhalation, you can feel the rush of energy through your torso. You can hold the air in your lungs and enjoy the stillness and the silence of the space between inhaling and exhaling. Next, you can exhale, feeling the air as it leaves your lungs and nostrils, this time as a warming movement of air through your body.

Practice an aware breath now.

There are many advanced breathing techniques that you can study. Again be sure that you have your goal in mind before you study them. A great book on this practice is *Light on Pranayama* by K. S. Iyengar.

Dancing is also a great path, although it is sometimes not as easy to focus on your goal as some other paths. Dancing can become a joyous action for the body/mind and when done with the goal of experiencing the Self in mind, it can lead you to your inner ecstasy. Just like the whirling dervishes who spin around and around in a controlled yet free manner, or as the participants dancing around a fire while chanting, as you dance, you should envision yourself merging with the object of your devotion. The Gopis dancing in joy to unite with Krishna; Sufis whirling in circles to unite with Allah. When you dance, move with the feeling that you are stripping away all misunderstanding of separation from your Self, and dance knowing you are one with the feeling within.

I found when I went out dancing, whether it was Friday night at a club, or Sunday morning in a gym posing as a dancing temple, as long as my focus was on the feeling of the Self within, my experience of dancing inevitably approached the ecstatic. It truly showed me the joy that is awaiting in all actions as the Self.

When you can perform this dance holding this high understanding, you can again recognize that your one-pointed focus towards your goal can carry you to the experience very quickly. If you can take the feeling into your daily life and have the experience beyond just your moments of dancing, this practice can lead you to knowing your inner Self as your truth.

One of the most powerful of all paths is the one described by Maharaj Nisargadatta, the path of one-pointed focus. As a householder, Nisargadatta did not have a lot of time during his day for practices. Instead he took one thing his Guru said and held onto it as tightly and as often as he could. His Guru told him that "You Are That." He decided that if he could just believe this statement and hold onto it, that it could carry him to the goal.

He trusted his Guru, he believed what he said, and he held the thought whenever he could, and after 3 years, he realized the complete truth of the statement. Instead of it being mere words, it had become a statement of the fact of his experience of life.

There is no difference between Maharaj and you, and this path is wide open for you to take to your goal.

Many actions can be used as helpers to release your belief in yourself as a tiny, separate entity, and to give you a glimpse of the Self within. Focusing on living in the present moment is a great practice. When you can do it in all the aspects of your life, you can attain your goal.

Visualizing yourself as an expansive being, allowing your awareness to grow beyond your body is another practice that quickly lets you see you are not who you once thought yourself to be.

When you understand that it is the Self that you are experiencing in the various practices you are performing, the need for formal practices can drop away. You can recognize that one of the main commonalities of all paths is that they start by making you aware of the inner Self, then they give you an experience of the feeling, and finally they show you how to get it. You recognize the common key in all. After that it is up to you to take your knowledge and experience and carry your learning into the world of your daily life.

If you can do this successfully, if you can understand that the practice is not an end in itself, but only an example of how to lead your life day after day, you will find whatever path you

choose to traverse will be short and sweet.

Chapter Fourteen: The Keys to the Pathless Path

If you have approached these descriptions with a discerning eye, you may begin to wonder. When you see the connections between all paths and have a good understanding of what enlightenment is, you may gradually recognize that you have a choice. "Will I follow one path, will I follow several paths, or will I just go to the goal?" you may ask yourself.

The tremendous reward of living and seeking enlightenment in the age of information is that there exist many people who have already walked these paths, and if we choose, we can learn from the experiences of others, and greatly reduce our efforts and the time it takes to reach our goal.

Having access to the teachings of many great teachers as well as the experiences of numerous seekers, we can recognize the commonalities between paths and distill the keys or most important points from each teaching. Understanding what is essential in each can lead us to a path or an understanding that will greatly circumvent the time seekers have historically dedicated to knowing their inner Self.

If we look at paths historically, we can see that great effort was the first ingredient that a seeker had to have in order to find a great Zen Master or a Guru. Many gurus were around, but few Gurus who could lead a person to realization were available. So a person had to invest a large amount of time and energy to even finding someone who had true information to impart.

From there, once the introductions were done, once a true teacher was found, and once the teacher agreed to accept the person as a student, the seeker had already established a mindset of belief that this was the way to enlightenment, since they would not have gone through all of the trouble they did if they did not believe it would work. Furthermore, they created within themselves a level of trust of the teacher, believing that he or she had reached a place of understanding that was deep and real, and that they had the power to transmit it from teacher to student.

So belief and trust in both the teacher and the path were paramount for a seeker to have on his or her journey towards realization. The mystique of having to have a special mantra given from teacher to disciple, the mystery of the awakening of the kundalini by the touch of a master, and the belief that one must have a Guru from a line of enlightened Gurus in order to attain enlightenment all further cemented the belief in a seeker that he or she had gone above and beyond the efforts of most other seekers to find their guide. Putting forth such an extreme effort undoubtedly meant that what they were receiving was special, unique and not only could but would produce results.

If all of these trappings did not make the seeker's mind into fertile ground for attaining realization, they moved on to the next teacher, again hopeful that all of these prerequisites were met and they could resonate with their teacher and believe the teaching could be received and followed to its goal. Some seekers could spend their whole lives travelling the globe trying to find the teacher who would fit the bill they had created in their minds. The mental noise can be endless when looking for a great teacher, and since we all imagine this teacher differently, the requirements we load onto this person can vary greatly. "He must be solemn and scholarly." "She must be light and accessible." "He must be a master of meditation." "She must be a yoga master, and she must be a good speaker." "I need to feel the peace of her presence." "He needs to have an aura that I can see." "I will just know it when I have met The One."

No wonder few seekers ever reached their goal when encountering the reality of most teachers. A Guru is one who has reached the understanding of their unity with the Self. This does not mean that they have let go of any of the idiosyncrasies of the person they previously thought themselves to be. If they were the type of person to laugh at everything before enlightenment, this personality trait would not disappear upon enlightenment. And if this was a trait you had known in flighty people during your lifetime, this teacher probably would not resonate with your belief system's needs for a Guru. It certainly does not mean that this Guru could not give you the understanding of enlightenment, but it does mean that you probably could not accept the teaching. Another Guru may have grown up in a society that believed in bathing once a week, or once a month, and your belief could be that a Guru must smell aromatic at all times, so again, you would not be in vibrational alignment with this teacher, and whatever she said, you could not accept with the level of belief necessary to carry you to the highest understanding. A Guru may have been an angry person, or even a deviant from the norms of society, and again, if he or she was too strange for you, you would not be open to receiving teachings from him or her.

Beyond the Guru, the teaching itself is set up in so many minds as being something that it is not, or at least does not have to be. Many of us have beliefs regarding the trials and tribulations that we must undergo to get the highest understanding. I remember a time when I thought in order to become enlightened I had to study for many years and understand all of the nuances of all the schools of yoga. I thought if I were able to spend many years living with a Guru, maybe I could attain enlightenment.

Many seekers will always move the bar just a little further out of their reach so whatever effort they are exerting is never quite enough. They can believe that those who have attained enlightenment are the special ones, and that they were specially marked even before enlightenment, and this specialness is something they lack.

Between building up the experience itself, the effort needed to get to it, and the person who one must be in order to attain anything, many seekers fall victim to a belief system that will never allow success. Many ashrams and centers of higher learning have an unspoken culture of belief that says the Guru is the only one who can be enlightened, the Guru is the only perfect one, and no one else can be enlightened, although we all must continue diligently on the path and hope for the grace to reach their exalted state one day. This underlying belief sets failure up as ultimately the only possible, realistic option for all but the most anointed of seekers.

Finally we set up so many different checkpoints along the way to help us believe we are walking the golden path toward enlightenment. We believe we need to see lights in our meditation, we think we must hear the mantra resonating within, we must see inner visions, and we must experience celestial beings dancing in our meditations. After enlightenment we must have other abilities, or we are not enlightened. "I must have all knowledge of the world, I must have miraculous powers to heal,

I must be able to go into people's dreams and transmit this understanding to them in their sleep."

No wonder very few of us are enlightened. With all the obstacles the mind throws up along the path, and with all the requirements it needs met in order to believe enlightenment has occurred, we are much like the hypnotized man who was told he would not be able to see his daughter upon leaving the trance. Even as she stood in front of him and he read a paper that the hypnotist held behind her, she was invisible to him. Or we are the man sitting on the old chest, oblivious to the fact that if he would just open it, a priceless treasure awaited within.

Even as we close in on the understanding that is enlightenment, we push it off and do not believe we could attain it. When we hold the understanding moments shy of it taking root in the core of our minds, we still can belittle ourselves in reference to this great attainment and convince ourselves that it really has got to be more, that I have got to do more, that I must believe it, I must experience it on a certain depth that I am not quite at yet. And we shrink from the understanding and always look for it out there, always a step or two away from our belief in our worthiness to attain it.

So if we really want to, we can begin our march to some far off Guru armed with a long list of beliefs which, when all met, will bring us to the brink of enlightenment, or we can understand that all of these things are part of a mindset that we can get immediately.

Choosing the latter, we see that these days we do not have to go to India to find a Guru. We don't even have to find a mountaintop in our own country. With a little help from the internet and a good book, we can read about the keys to the great ancient teachings. We can ready ourselves to receive their fruit, and we can scale the mountain to its height in moments.

As in the example of Nisargadatta's path at the end of the last chapter, we can see three essential ingredients to attaining realization: belief, trust and focus. We can see the historical set up of Guru and disciple took care of belief for the truly sincere seeker. They believed in the Guru, they believed in the teachings, and they believed they could have the ultimate understanding mystically transferred. If they stayed with the Guru, and if they were able to see past the differences between what they believed a Guru should be and what they saw standing before their eyes, then they had a basis for trust. If the teachings resonated within as true to their beliefs, then trust was established. Focus was addressed when the dedicated disciple would give up a worldly life to be with the Guru. They would then give all of their time and energy to the attainment of this goal. If they could keep their focus on what was at hand, then they could truly learn from their teacher.

Nisargadatta believed in his Guru, kept his trust in his Guru and he put his focus on the Guru's words, all in his spare time. In a time when people believed they had to spend time at the Guru's feet, he was able to train himself to believe he had gotten all that he needed from the Guru in one sentence, and he trusted that a physical representation of the Guru was not needed in his daily life for him to attain the highest understanding. He took himself from a shopkeeper to a realized being with only belief, trust and focus. Who of us cannot do the same?

On this pathless path, you must have belief in the possibility of enlightenment coming to you now. You must honestly believe it is not something just for someone else, somewhere else, but it is here for you right now.

You must trust in the words of the masters throughout history. They all have said the same thing: "You are God." I use a lot of words to talk about various aspects of this Self, including Void, Unmanifest, Emptiness, Peace, Being. Any one of these words may resonate better with you and have less baggage than "God", and may have great meaning for you. Maybe simply "I Am That," or "So' ham" is in tune with your vibrational frequency.

If you can put your trust in anyone, a realized being seems to be a good place to start. If they all say tell you the same thing, then it is probably true. Jesus said it with words that were possibly easier to digest, "The Kingdom of Heaven lies within," but the meaning was no less powerful. Ramana Maharshi put it this way "Awareness...that I am."

Hold onto the expression of this truth that means the most to you.

If you can latch onto what enlightened beings say, if you can focus on it internally, then you can use it like a koan in Zen and allow it to unfold its deep meaning in your mind and experience through the practice of one-pointed focus. Holding onto your person statement of truth, believing it has the power to take you to realizing your Self, and continuing to focus on it, returning to it again and again until you really have it is the key to take you to the final realization of your identity with the Self of all within.

If your mind wants still more to chew on, you should be able to look at the various practices listed previously and see that the common thread running through them all is the feeling of Self and becoming the witness or increasing your awareness of this feeling within. You chant, and meditate and do service and contemplate all to have this inner feeling, and to basically exercise your Self-recognition muscle within. You are doing what is essentially a spiritual workout, the goal of it being the sculpting of a muscle that is the awareness of the fullness of the Self within. As you work this muscle doing your exercise of choice, you begin to see that what you once thought was different than you, what you once placed on a pedestal far above you is actually what you are. With this self-recognition comes a letting go of your former beliefs and an acceptance of what is real in your experience. Whereas before you identified yourself as a person and you were listening with your ego-muscle, you now identify as the Self, which you have been introduced to and realize is with you always, and with everyone, as everyone, always.

Basically you are changing an understanding, but it takes an awful lot of effort to change the most basic understanding that we grow up with and live most of our lives with unquestioning. While it is easy for me to teach you what 1 + 1 is now, many years ago before you knew it, it seemed a difficult concept to learn. The fact which makes it pretty easy to add to your list of concepts is that you did not have an opposing concept or a mistaken experience telling you something different.

If I told you the world is best modeled as a hologram, you might have much more resistance because science has not decided on this unequivocally yet, and previously you have learned a different belief. Learning something new like this is much like the case of people who were told the earth is round, after living a life believing otherwise. This new thought went against their long-held belief and was not easily switched. With more evidence I could better convince you that a holographic model fits better than a wave-particle description, and you may begin to agree, but only after a lot of evidence, and a lot of study.

It is not so different with realization, although the tools used to convince you of this truth are a bit different. Instead of scientific proof, we have the words of the saints and sages throughout history. Instead of study, you have your inner experience. You have the feeling of me within that you know and love and recognize as yourself, and you are being guided to have this same feeling slowly re-identified as the Self that is within all and which is not personal, but universal.

If you can stick with this study, examining and experiencing the feeling, you will begin to see that it takes on a life of its own inside your mind. Much like other difficult subjects, a higher understanding comes just from holding onto a thought.

When you are learning a new subject, you study, then you put it down and you go to sleep. The next day you find it has gone deeper into your psyche and you understand it more.

The same is true of a new ability. Allowing the subconscious part of your mind to do its work is the surest way to learn anything. It is no different with learning that you are not a person, but the universal Self of all. You sit and study it consciously, the subconscious mind works with it while you sleep, and one day it clicks. The more effort your conscious mind gives to learning, the larger the impression on your subconscious mind, and the faster it will be in understanding something new.

Once you understand "intellectually" then you have it. "But it is just an intellectual understanding," you may reply.

What other type of understanding exists? If understanding doesn't occur in the intellect, where does it occur?

"But I want to experience it," you may say to clarify.

What are you doing with each breath, but experiencing the Self within? The same feeling of self that previously you thought of as a person is now the feeling of Self that is the Being of all. When this feeling comes into contact with the mind, it takes on the feeling of Self, but it is really just Being. It feels like "I am," when it is experienced in our life, but it is really just I when we strip it down to its essential feeling. At its deepest point it is not even an "I", but only a feeling of beingness, nothing more.

When you stop adding various beautiful trappings onto your understanding, you can go beyond the mystique that you have made for it to be. When you let go of the last of your beliefs, you will find that what you are left with was what you started with. The you that was there at the beginning is the same you that is there at the culmination of your search. The one big difference is the name that you give yourself. Before you were the person with a life and actions and thoughts and feelings; now you are Creation and the Unmanifest and the Self that all share, unbeknownst to most minds. Before you were the ocean thinking you were a drop; now you are the ocean knowing you are the ocean experiencing yourself as each drop.

Before, you were Clark Kent. You spin around a little and your identity changes and now you are Superman. Your identification has changed from a mistaken one to a real one. That's all.

The less fantastical you can make this switch appear as in your mind, the easier it becomes. Once you are on the other side of it, you can immediately start to see what before was nonsense, and what previously seemed contradictory, now will make complete sense. Zen koans are easy to answer. Non-dual understanding becomes clear. You are nothing and everything, empty and full simultaneously. It is not by magic that clarity and answers come, but simply by a change in perspective. When you are seeing the sky believing you are a cloud, you think differently than when you are experiencing the sky knowing you are the sky seeing through the eyes of a cloud.

You created your limitations with your old beliefs, and you transcended them with your new understanding/experience. The mind really does create the world, and it does so on many levels including how it sees itself as a limited Self. As soon as you experience your Self through your practice, and feel that

Self in another and recognize that same feeling is actually inside of you. Whereas before you limited the feeling to the person you thought you were, now you allow it to be as it really is and it expands to include all of Creation. It is in the saint to whom you were devoted, in the guy sitting of the street corner, in your lover, and in that woman who says the silliest things on tv every day. The people haven't change; the only difference is that the understanding in your head has finally come to make total sense. Now you see clearly.

In the end you believed and trusted in the greatest teachings, and you believed and trusted that you were worthy to understand and experience them. You focused on experiencing that truth within, and recognized that what you previously thought was only you was actually everyone. Depending on how long you choose to believe and experience your self as your

Self, enlightenment can occur in the next moment, or the next lifetime.

It is all up to your mind and which experience you will allow it to create.

Chapter Fifteen: What Is the Nature of Reality?

If the body is really a spacesuit for the Soul to live on this planet, then the mind is a filter allowing the Soul to experience a particular slice of an infinite movie. It is much like going to a movie theater, and being given a pair of 3D glasses. The difference is that at this theater there is only one screen and your 3D glasses also have earphones. And when you get the glasses/headphones there are many different ones to choose from and each allows for a different movie to be seen on the one screen. Those of us who share this vibrational experience are viewers of the movie we could call Earth 2014 Revision 0. Others could be sitting right next to us watching Earth 2014 Revision 1, or Earth 2020 Revision 0, or even Earth Level 12 Revision 0. The possibilities are endless.

On top of all of this, the basic reality of what we are experiencing and sharing on our Earth 2014 is that we are on a fast moving spaceship. Between the rotational speed of the earth, the rotation of the Earth around the Sun, the motion and rotation of the Sun around the galactic center, and the speed of the Milky Way through the cosmos, at every moment of our lives we are moving at approximately 2 million miles an hour, or 3.2 million km/hr relative to an unmoving point in space.

If the timeless, still silent Self is the unmoving background, akin to what we think of as space itself, then the planets and stars and galaxies are literally the three dimensional movie dancing across the screen that is the Self. In each moment, Creation is flitting across the screen that is the Self or the Void, enlivening the Self that moments before was dark and peaceful experiencing itself, and which will again a moment later return to its peace. Viewed this way the Self in each moment is a new point having the opportunity to be what has been created on its screen for a passing nanosecond. It chooses to limit itself, to become part of a star, a planet, a person, an air molecule, then returning to itself, the Source of all, the Unmanifest, the Void, ready to be veiled again into another manifest form for another moment.

Can the mind really begin to grasp all of this? No wonder the mind instead paints the picture of a world that most of us share, albeit from a plethora of perspectives. Each mind experiencing this world sees it differently. A chair to me may be a basic wooden chair while the same word may conjure a different picture in your head. My fork could be a certain size and shape, while yours, although existing in the same family may look quite different. Multiply this by the 5 or 10,000 words we each have in our vocabularies, and you can see we each live in our own individual worlds. Our experiences, our place in our families, our society, our place in that society, our culture, all of these things add to the inputs that make us see the world through slightly different eyes. And it is not just seeing a world, but creating a world that we end up doing. The way we see the world colors how we react to it, and how we believe it is treating us, so each of us is, daily, living in and making different worlds.

The same is true of spirituality. A one size fits all religion does not exist. I say "Jesus," and the name immediately will create a million different pictures in a million different heads. Each different, each with its own attachments and beliefs. Many words in religion are especially loaded with various meanings and connotations, and create problems more often than facilitating communication. Two Catholics who sit next to each other every week for mass practice and experience two different forms of Catholicism. They can coexist, of course, but make no mistake, they are different. The same is true for all other religions and schools of thought. There is just no way for two people to have the exact same understanding of anything. Close enough to understand and relate, yes; the same, no.

When we speak of realization, this is why we see so many different paths towards the goal. And if we understand it in this new light, we can see that each one of us is actually creating his or her own spiritual path. Each one of us has the right to write a book on how they came to understand the world the way they do, and all of these books would help others coming up to reach their goals.

It is always helpful to see things from multiple viewpoints. If you look at an elephant from one perspective, you will not know an elephant well. If you take numerous vantage points and add the information together, then you can know the elephant much better. The same is true of your spiritual path. When you walk along and listen to guidance from others who have walked a similar path, you can better understand the things you are experiencing, especially if you keep in mind that what they saw will at best be similar, but not identical to what you are seeing. If you can learn from their insights, you can traverse the path all the merrier. If you can take the advice of others who are walking to the same goal, even on other paths, you can appreciate how similar we all are, despite the outward differences, and you can learn from those experiencing other paths.

If I hear someone talking about Jesus, I can hear someone who has put an intermediary between themselves and God. Or I can hear someone who has recognized the Self in Jesus, which Jesus realized. I can hear someone who knows this Self or Christ within is within us all, and is known by various names in various traditions. When they speak of Jesus' love, I can hear the love of the Guru, or Universal Love, or I can hear anything that helps me to better relate to the high experience of love that they are having.

It is much more helpful for me to understand the way someone sees things in a light that is useful and empowering, than to see it in a manner that is critical or condescending. It helps me walk my path in an uplifting manner knowing that others around me use different language as they walk to the same ultimate goal. We are not alone on our journey back to the Source, even if we all are the Source, playing a multitude of roles, walking back to our home.

So we can see that reality is a shifting sand under our feet, never the same for any two people, always similar, always close enough to find common ground. It is shaped by our minds, and by our beliefs. It is never small enough to fit into a box the mind can make for it.

More and more scientists are postulating that the world as we live in it can be described in a manner similar to the description of a hologram. When we look at this thought through the lens of ancient teachings, we can believe that maybe scientists are beginning to see the same thing that seers throughout history have experienced while in higher states of consciousness. The substance of the world is ethereal or illusory, and the stuff of this plane of existence only has form to those whose senses are attuned to it. Seen from the perspective of the Source, all is Maya. Seen from the perspective of realization, form is doing nothing but playing with itself. Scientists can see this same world as waves of varying frequency.

As deep as science can take us, it has been theorized by a few that the essence of all can be seen in each part, which shows the true holographic nature of this reality. This is again the same as sages and even psychics have experienced in deep states, seeing that everything is interconnected and the whole can be known in the grain of sand. This all points back to the

Void or Unmanifest at each point being the whole of existence, the entire play, just awaiting its cue to play a particular role. As the rolling play of the galaxy passes each particular point in Void/Space, the spotlight shines on the Beingness, bringing it into Creation for a moment, allowing it to shine as a pixel in this divine play before going dark again, going from its moment as the Manifest, to again rest as the peace of the Unmanifest.

Chapter Sixteen: What Is the Nature of the Mind?

It is very important to be clear about the nature of the mind. Our experience of the world goes through our mind. In fact the way we see the life we are living is created by the mind, so understanding mind is imperative to understanding life.

All of the aforementioned paths are greatly assisted when the mind is an active participant in understanding the meaning behind the actions and the commonalities involved in the various paths. Enlightenment itself is of the mind. The body does not become enlightened; the mind experiences enlightenment. There is not a wave of energy or a bolt of light, but only the acceptance and true understanding of an identity.

Just as the mind goes through life thinking, "I am a baby," then "I am a girl," then "I am a big girl," then "I am a teenager," then "I am an adult," then "I am a teacher," then "I am a wife," then "I am a mother," then "I am a volunteer," then "I am a grandmother," then "I am a retiree," then can be, "I am enlightened." When the last thought is the identity, the I falls away since the understanding contained in enlightenment is the ending of being someone. The thought, "Enlightenment has occurred here," replaces it, but it is still a thought in the mind.

The mind has many different contributing factors to what we sloppily know as "thinking". The yogis have identified several different types of thought, and at one time I was able to breakdown the various types of thought into 11 different categories. Mankind has believed that each individual brain produces what we know as thought, but there are some who believe the mind is more a receiver than a thinker, receiving the thoughts that are on the particular frequency at which you are living and vibrating.

The mechanism of thought can be seen to have several threads which exist in the past, present or future, as well as in a mode of examining and of fantasizing. If you are deep in meditation you can perceive that these different types of thoughts appear to arise from different places, or they are received in different areas of the brain, and they are transmitted to the active thought "pipeline" independent of one another. You may have the mantra, or a song stuck in your head, repeating over and over in the background, and in the foreground you have your intellect telling you some brilliant understanding. Both happen at once, but the pipeline of attention will only allow one thought through at a time, so they alternate, taking turns flashing into your consciousness.

This subtle observation is another way to see that there is not one person or awareness behind the mind, but that mind is a tool of the Awareness that you are.

Although connected to the brain, mind does not have a physical basis. It can be said that mind is nothing but the current thought. When the thought ceases, so does the mind. The energy that is reserved from consciousness for the mind either goes to thinking the next thought, or it goes into the feeling of consciousness that exists behind thought. When the energy of the mind believes it is a person, it uses the energy to manifest thoughts. When it believes it is the Self, mind has the choice to think, or to remain still and feel the energy of Beingness within.

The enlightened mind does not value every thought as highly as the unenlightened one. It understands that thoughts are clouds in the sky of the mind, and it lets them float on.

As I am not one who believes in order to throw the garbage out, you must go through each little piece of it and examine it before discarding it, I do not think looking at all of the pieces of the mind, including dissecting the ego is a worthwhile use of time. It is enough to know the mind values itself most highly though, as is evidenced by the feelings of ego that it entertains. It loves to think, and loves to believe its thoughts are the most useful ones ever to take shape, and has no doubt that it is always right. Meditation helps us see this propensity of the mind, and the energy of stillness is enough to cleanse this habitual way of life for the mind if we stay true to our practice.

The mind has been labeled the monkey mind, and when it is not being vain, it is just talking, just singing a song, or just keeping your attention in any direction it has decided is more interesting than living in the present moment. The mind really believes that its conversations are more interesting than living, so it runs them non-stop. Much like a television set that believes it is best for the people in the house that it is always on, the mind will run without purpose in lieu of allowing you to experience the sights and sounds and feelings that are currently happening to you.

Far be it for the mind to let you feel good for more than a minute or two. It loves drama and will look to the next problem, creating one when there isn't one, and blowing one up in importance when there are minor issues in your daily life. The unexamined mind also does not ever want to rest in contentment, so it will turn pseudo-philosophical asking, "What is the meaning of my life?" only to send itself on a wild goose chase, usually one that ends up not feeling so good by the end.

The universe is an amazing creation, but on the level we are aware of, the level of body and mind, certain questions can only be asked, but never satisfactorily answered. While life is seen as a play of Creation from the enlightened perspective, a play that has no meaning except for the fun of playing itself, for the mind that asks for purpose, there is an assumption that there is an individual who wants this answer and who must accomplish a certain something. So the question is asked from a completely wrong perspective, and yet it still demands to be answered. Much like asking, "Why does the ocean fly into the sky every night?" There is no ocean that does that, so to ask why it does it is pointless; similarly there is no person living a life, so to ask, "What is the meaning of my life," is pointless.

If we understand the foibles of the mind, then we will not allow it to drag us down into its pits. If we can instead take a lighter view of its activities, we can let it lead us to enjoying the fun in all of the moments of life instead of demanding that the world around us shape itself to our whims. We can see it when it performs, and laugh at what it thinks. Eventually we will experience it taking itself less seriously, and appreciating the stillness that allows mind to cease and Consciousness to arise. Then mind becomes the friend of the piece of Creation that you are, and life has a gentle, peaceful feel to it; an inner joy dances in your experiences instead of overtones of constant confrontation and continual dissatisfaction.

In your search for understanding, the mind is both the greatest foe and the most important tool. It will happily take you off on a tangent that may take years of your time, all so that it can continue having the "fun" it believes it is having in the form of the immersion in the drama of life. It will distract you at every turn as it feels itself coming closer to change. But it is also indispensable in making the connections necessary to reaching that final understanding.

The fact that it does so unwillingly is ultimately nothing but the play of Creation. Just as Creation veils itself to play with itself, it has made the process of unveiling exciting and uses the mind to keep the game fun. If it were easy, the game would already be over, and that is not how Creation is playing its game. So instead it uses the mind as both the villain and the hero, the creator of turmoil and the seer of truth. Just as the mind is the tool that creates all the intricacies that you worry about all through the day, it also creates the connections that enlighten you. It is nothing less than incredible that Creation uses the mind in these ways. Who could write a thriller with a more amazing protagonist/antagonist than Creation itself has with each mind?

When the mind cares too deeply about something, it creates an impression that you come back to again and again. Life is really not meant to be dwelled upon or obsessively relived, so when the tool of experience, the mind, is misused into thinking some action or experience is terribly important, it has a difficult time moving on from it. Much like the song that you may not even like which gets stuck in your head, the mind repeats events over and over for no reason other than the importance you assign to it.

When you are living a life understanding praise and blame are two sides of the same coin, and when you value the peace and stillness that are the home feelings for the Self within, you do not allow the mind to establish impressions or get into grooves that it must think about over and over. You do not worry so much about opinions that others have given to you, positive or negative. You understand that they have minds that want to share an opinion in order to feel important. You now see that you do not have to play inside of that game anymore.

Songs with meaningless lyrics do not hold as much interest as they used to, and dramas with indelible images do not have the same pull to be watched as they did before. Even the thrill of watching competition, a major pastime of this society, does not mean as much to you. The peaceful mind does not look to be entertained in ways that once used up hours of time.

The ups and downs of daily life will try to pull the mind into their game, and at times they will succeed. Sometimes things seem so important. Certain things must be taken care of, certain duties and tasks obviously need to be fulfilled, but they should not jerk the mind permanently away from peace. When you allow yourself to forget, the mind that stays inside of an issue in life is a mind that has forgotten the joy of the Self, and how everything works out exactly the way Creation plans.

Although being mired deep in the drama may seem more fun for a short while, to the mind, it needs to be reminded that the posture of witness is much truer than that of gilded participant.

Understanding the nature of the mind, and understanding the way it behaves is much like understanding what gravity does: it will pull you down to the lowest point if left to operate without awareness. When you meditate, when you breathe remembering your Self, you help the mind to go to a higher level. You remind it that it is your tool of enlightenment. You let it be the best that it can be.

Your mind can be likened to a dog's nose. You can allow it to follow its base instinct and it will chase tail after tail after tail. Or you can train it to sniff out a certain smell of your choosing. It will then use its one-pointed focus to take you unerringly towards your goal.

You choose which path you are on, and allow your mind the priorities you choose.

When you are vigilant with what you feed your mind and watchful of how you allow the mind to engage with the world, you are experiencing Creation living through you in a purified manner. You are not flung back and forth by the monkey mind reacting to the world, but are instead choosing the path you walk. Although all is truly Creation, you understand that certain parts of Creation can generally take you to knowing your Self faster than other parts, and you tune into the beauty and joy that Creation hides awaiting our recognition. While the saint and the beggar can be one and the same, more often than not, the saint will lead you to the state you are seeking a bit faster than the beggar, although they are both players of Creation. Their roles usually differ and the direction each leads a person towards on a path differs.

Simply put, without understanding, the mind is the worst of all enemies; with understanding the mind can be our greatest friend. We choose how we use it afresh in each moment.

Chapter Seventeen: Life on the Other Side of Enlightenment

Realization is for the mind. It is nothing but the Manifest or Creation saying "I want to have a clear experience of myself at this point, at this here/now." When the mind can see the reality of its place in existence without creating a person, there is a lightness behind all actions. Life is suddenly not so serious, but more of a game. The nature of the play can be seen and enjoyed, even as you continue to play your role. Just as an actor on set can remember his real life as he says the lines of his character, so too does the enlightened being remember the Self of all even as she picks up the kids from school.

The life of an enlightened person throughout history has been one of a saint or monk living apart from society with the occasional saint venturing into the masses to teach the good news of reality. As we enter an age where more people are in touch with and ready for enlightened teachings, more of us are experiencing the final realization as we live lives of householders. We have families, we have jobs, and we have money problems and health issues and all the other things that come with the Maya of this lifetime. Through all of this, we still connect to the truth remembering who we really are.

We meditate in the morning or evening and connect with pure Being, then we slide down into the realm of Creation and live as part of the whole, performing our duty or our dharma in our lives. We may go chanting, we may do japa, we may perform service, or go to church. We may do none of these things.

Any action performed by the person we were before we realized we were not really a person, we may still find the mind and body continuing to do. As the watcher of it all, there is no judgment of any action, so we do it and appreciate the fruit of the action. Our inner experience of it is the only real change. We are not seeking anything from the action, but instead we are enjoying the journey.

We have already reached the ultimate goal, so all the rest is just enjoyment of the continuing experience of life.

As contemplation was always my mind's favorite practice, contemplation continues. New realizations on how to see the world, and new perspectives on the experience of reality arise almost daily. Much like walking around a mountain and describing its top from the vantage point of each step, the contemplative mind can see new and amazing ways to describe the Ultimate every day.

Every day is like a journey from the top of the mountain around the flora and fauna it has to offer. As you walk down from the peak into your daily life, if you want to experience love, you hop off the trail where you can see the goal as love. If you want to experience joy, you step off the path where everything is clearly full of light and joy. If you want to laugh more, you go to the spot of amusement, and laugh till it hurts, all in the playful glee of the Self. Or if you want to bask in the peace of the Self, you go to the place marked Peace.

Sometimes we don't realize that this choice from the part of ourselves that has created all of this even exists, and we find ourselves experiencing Void/Space. It is empty and even can feel barren and to the mind it can feel useless or bleak. When we find ourselves in this spot, we again must see that that is where we got off the path, and if that is not how we want to view the mountaintop, we have the choice to move on, to go to a

place that is much more pleasant for the mind.

In the end we must remember that this play of forms and

all of the feelings and daily experiences and even realization

itself are all for the mind, and if the mind wants to feel good, then

it can choose to do so very easily. The Unmanifest, or Void or

Self, which we experience in its varied shades does not care

about what mind may feel. The mind in the here/now is the only

one who cares about a given feeling in a given moment, and it is

the sole arbiter of its state. The mind truly creates the world it

lives in, and the realized mind is a mind trained to remember this

and to practice actions that nurture thoughts (or the no-thought

state) which feel good. Why would it consciously choose

otherwise, unless it is bored, curious or acting from karma or

dharma? Then when it is not bored anymore, it can remember to return to a better place. When the karma is burnt up or the dharma completed, it returns to an empowered choice.

So we continue to live as we did before on the outside, and on the inside, we have a space of joy and truth that we are always connected to. Just as before you took for granted that you were a person, now you take for granted that you are the Universal Being behind all. A simple little shift in understanding, but a powerful change in the way you see the things of your world. No longer do the big things in your daily experience matter so much. You know you are behind everything, you are good, and everything will work out as it should. You can enjoy the journey now, understanding that the journey and the goal are one.

You don't fear living as you once did, and you don't fear death. You understand since you are not the body, you were not born a few years ago, and you will not die a few years from now.

You are Being before time, and the feeling of I that you love so will always exist, as long as there is life in the universe. The feeling of pure beingness that is inside the feeling of I will exist always. As you feel it now, you can intuit that there is no endpoint in front of it or behind it. The feeling just is; beingness is eternal.

Like the clouds in the sky, each body in the world has its short moment, then it is gone. And like the sky, what was there before the clouds, what sustained the clouds, and what remains after they are gone, the Being we really are makes and supports all of Creation, and remains after Creation ceases. It is an amazing shift to go from being a cloud to being the whole of the sky; the same is true with the shift realization brings, taking us from body/mind identification to Being/Space awareness.

While the mind that now has this understanding is still in one place, experiencing the life of one body, it has become one of the minds of the universe, seeing things from a universal perspective, understanding things for the Beingness that is beyond thinking as we know it. As you now contemplate life, you are not a person thinking about what you want to have happen in your life, but you are the universe, enjoying the play of the stars, the planets, and the people on the planets –including their emotions, deeds and desires.

You are not willing things to be good for the person you once thought yourself to be, but you are happy that life is good for all of creation. You are manifesting at each moment each activity of the universe, not just the new car the body you find yourself inside might want. None of the manifesting asks for the assistance of the mind/body you are in, either, except maybe for the manifestation of things in the life of which your mind is

aware. Even this assent is actually only Creation manifesting

what it wants to experience at the body/mind that you formerly

thought of as me.

From the outside, life before enlightenment and after

enlightenment are very similar. On the other hand, on the inside

the experience of life changes dramatically. Life from an

enlightened perspective differs from a normal life in it lightness.

When you believe you are a person who must do certain things

in order to live a life in a certain way, you create a lot of stress.

When instead the understanding exists that Creation is playing

its game and you are witnessing it as that which created,

supports and is throughout it all, then there exists in your

awareness an inner confidence that there is nothing to worry

about, that everything works out as Creation has decided. There

is a trust that Creation knows what is best, and will take the body/mind that you are experiencing through the most beneficial path to the various trials of life.

On the outside, you still have to stand in line at a grocery store. There is no express lane for the enlightened. So as you stand there holding your basket, you still feel the pain of your muscles as you switch hands to hold the 25 pounds of groceries you have crammed into the little basket, but there is not a complainer inside your head anymore. At least not one to whom you believe and listen. You may hear "Why do I always get into the slowest line?" in your head, then you may laugh knowing the thought is a remnant of the person you used to think you were. Previously the thought fueled your growing anger about the unfairness of life, but now it shows you the little moments that make up this funny play we all experience.

Or if you are tuned into the moment, you feel your muscles burn. You listen to the voices around you. You enjoy the expanded space of the high ceilings in the store, feeling your consciousness filling the entire space. You enjoy the colors and the smells and the play of life in a grocery store as it happens this afternoon. On the outside others see a person standing, possibly differing only by the tiny smile on the lips of the enlightened you, or the twinkle in the eyes.

You could even choose to play the role of the person totally at that moment, and those tiny cues of an inner shift would be non-existent. From the inside you would behave as you did before enlightenment, with only the smallest hint of the knowing you now have sitting in the back of your mind.

However you choose to live the moment, it is a choice the Universe makes at the spot that is the body/mind you intimately experience, and this awareness is always there the moment you look to it.

Life has changed, and life is the same, and life will never ever be the same, all rolled up into one. And enlightenment helps you to understand how all of this is joyfully true.

Chapter Eighteen: What Are Creation and Being?

At its purest, Being is Unmanifest or Void. It knows only itself. As it veils itself or as it changes its frequency or as it begins this world, it becomes Awareness. It knows itself in relation to itself and in relation to ways it is limiting itself. As it limits itself more, it becomes Creation, or the Manifest, then it is known as Life and the Self. At each level, the Unmanifest is seeing itself through different lenses or at different vibrational frequencies, but it is still the Unmanifest from the vantage point of the Void. It is all the Self, from that more limited vantage point. From the vantage point of the person, it is me and them. All is still the One, but seen through very limited eyes and understanding, the Unmanifest appears to really be a bunch of people. This is called Maya, and this is nothing but the play of Creation.

Not long ago, my son took a piece of paper and cut a spiral circle around the edge slowly going towards the center with each turn. The Unmanifest sees the paper while it is flat. It contains everything and is undifferentiated in its fullness. Creation sees the same paper unfolded, spiraling open from top to bottom, manifesting as different sizes and shapes at different levels and seen from different perspectives. One perspective could be labeled Peace, and other Joy, and other Bliss. All the opposites exist from the vantage points available to Creation, and none are manifest when seen from the Void.

If you are needing a supreme being that is separate from his creation, you won't find it. You can believe in it all you want, but until you open your perspective up to include yourself in the creation and before you stop limiting your picture of your god and instead allow God to be one with all of creation and to be an intimate part of it all, knowing all because it is all, you won't really know a God beyond the one created and misunderstood by man. Nothing, including any god is separate from the whole of Creation, which is continually creating, sustaining and destroying itself, only to begin anew in each moment of its play.

Various explanations of how the world really is are like each of us seeing a portion of the coastline and believing that which we see as describing the whole. We believe the coast moving in then out is the only way it is and it is the totality. When someone else says it is different, we do not believe them and at times we even fight to show them we are right and they are wrong.

If instead we could see that as far as what we focused on in viewing the coast, we were right, just as what they focused on in their viewing makes them right. If you add the two together, you can more than likely get a much clearer picture of much more of the coast than you could with just one or the other

description.

The Void is the Self is the Unmanifest is Emptiness is

Space. The totality of the Holographic Multiverse is folded onto

itself and exists as totally full Void. From the perspective of

people, it is void, it is empty; from the perspective of the Void, it

is full and vibrant. From the differentiated point of view it is

barren; from the vantage point of the Void it is completely full of

the totality of all possibility at each point and in each moment in

all realities.

It unfolds itself into the universe of galaxies and stars

and planets and people and animals and insects and minerals,

veiling itself with each step away from its totality. It is Unmanifest

in that it is the totality of all manifestation only without the choice

being made of the manifestation at each point. It is pure

potentiality, brimming with all potentials. Like a full mass of matter which opens up and folds out to expose an intricate, delicate latticework of creation, the Unmanifest contains all awaiting to be known in the world of Creation.

The Self is felt and identified as this Void at the intersection of body/mind and the Void. It is felt as a self by the body/mind which in its ignorance mistakes pure Being, which is the Void, as a person.

From the perspective of the Void, there is only Void. This needs to be clearly understood. All the rest that is Creation is experienced by Creation and the Self, but the Void, the purest, the Absolute, knows only itself as itself. No matter what the form, the Void only knows the Void. From the perspective of Creation there exists the seer, the seen and seeing.

The finest particle or vibration or piece of space can only see and know itself. It cannot see a more complex particle or vibration. The bigger the particle gets, the larger and more differentiated the panorama of its vista becomes. The eye of man can see the macrocosm. The eye of a telescope can see a larger macrocosm, while a microscope can see a microcosm. The same is true of the Void and Creation. The fine Void can know only itself, while Creation in its myriad forms can know the immense variety of itself, although in the end it must be remembered that there is no difference, and all is the Unmanifest, although it is playing a game for a time as the Manifest.

We live in Creation as the Created. We are not separate from Creation, but are an integral part, a complete whole at each part. Creation or the Universe is the doer. The Awareness we see the world through is the witness of it all. I may feel there is a me that can do something, but from a higher perspective, there is only Creation making things happen at each place and at each time. Even the way you feel and react and think are part of the whole of Creation, not independent individual acts. We are truly part of a gigantic, interactive, complex play, all of whose parts have been written out, and what we witness every day is our play.

It is easy to say that the Universe controls everything, does everything, and is all that we see and know and do. It is much more challenging for the ego-absorbed mind to believe or even to want to believe this. The mind always wants to believe it has control, that there is a person who is doing, and that what I do is important. The mind wants to think that it has autonomy, that there is such a thing as free will.

If the mind needs this thought, and if it does not interfere with the dharma of the part that you are playing in this grand production, then go right ahead and think it. Who chose to think it anyway actually?

If you feel better believing you have some say in the actions of the life that you are really just the witness and support of, then believe.

If you feel better thinking that it is all just happening around you and you have nothing to do with it, then believe this. Whichever empowers your mind most is most valuable. If believing you have no say in things depresses your mind, then don't think this way. If believing you can change things and make the world a better place stresses you out, then don't believe it.

Creation is in charge, doing the doing, thinking and acting, happening all around itself always, so you can believe how you want, but it is only Creation believing it, really.

Whatever you think will shape the experience you have of your world, so make sure to choose empowering thoughts that make your mind feel bliss. In reality everything is just happening, without one volitional doer, with the entire Manifestation as the doer always. Since this thought can be too big and too out of control for many minds, the Manifestation will choose for individual minds to believe otherwise, to believe they have choice, and this belief, from the Universe, helps the Universe to move exactly as it wants at each given point. We don't even have the will to decide to empower ourselves, ultimately, but as part of the play, we need to believe we do, so motion continues.

If you really want to believe you can control something, stop thinking for five minutes right now.

Could you do it? If not, then you see how much control over the mind a supposed "you" has?

If you could, then thanks, you have done just what the Universe wanted you to do, following the suggestion that it wrote in these pages long ago. Either way you can at the very least come to the conclusion that the mind can never really see where volition is coming from, and will never totally believe there is no possibility of free will.

It is the nature of Creation's creation to be this way.

So Creation does everything, and Self is the only "I" in the Universe. Before the feeling of Self arises, there is only Being, and before even that feeling lies the Void. All names represent the same thing, all different aspects, different faces of the Absolute, each term emphasizing a role or a texture of the Absolute. We should not get confused by the names or by the delineations that may be placed on the aspects of the Unmanifest. In the end, we are all just this One, unfolded and playing as game, watcher and watched. There is separation from the viewpoint of the game, but only unity from the understanding eye of the Absolute. As Creation speeds across our surface and through our space, for a moment it flashes loud and colorful, then it is gone and Peace reigns supreme again.

Creation has appeared on and in the Unmanifest. If Creation were to cease, the Unmanifest would still be the Unmanifest, the seed of all possibilities, unaware of any of them. The Unmanifest is the source of Creation, but Creation just happens. Only to the created does there appear to be a sense of order and meaning. The created needs a sense of purpose, a sense of individual self, and the concurrent struggle between the opposites of good/bad, happy/sad, and love/hate. This creates the drama that gives life its juice, and makes the individual feel alive.

Transcending this is what enlightenment is about and it may not appeal to some, although we all are inherently seeking its fruit. We all crave freedom, and we yearn for love and happiness, the calling cards of the Self. Every day we seek these things, not realizing it is the one feeling of Beingness within us all for which we are searching.

So we prefer to stay wrapped inside the pull of the opposites instead of breaking free and having all the understanding that goes with this freedom. "It is great to know Peace, but not necessarily fun to give up being a person." "It is fine to know the Self, but what about the joy of drama?" How many of us enjoy a good cry every now and then? So yes we can see how the opposites have a hold on many of us, and until their play becomes too monotonous or too painful, we will continue seeking the good and accepting the bad instead of choosing to go beyond both.

Ultimately this is exactly what Creation has chosen and is doing, as it gives us these desires and plays with us through them.

You are the puppet master putting on a show, and as you do so, you begin thinking you are one of your characters, all the while continuing to control them all. One day you will remember again, and until that time you will play your game and enjoy the highs and suffer the lows of the character you believe you are. When you remember, it will be as if you have awakened, and you will probably decide to put on another play.

For the person who has been created, thought continues to support beliefs. Mind creates a person and when enlightenment comes, mind stops believing in this person. The total meaning and usefulness of enlightenment is to allow the mind to see life differently. Whereas before enlightenment many occurrences in life brought stress and unease, after enlightenment, knowing the identity of the background, there is an ease and a lightness that takes over in these same situations, and overall life becomes a joy.

Creation has basically chosen a particular mind through which it can clearly experience life and living in the moment when enlightenment occurs. So the mind that once thought of itself as a "me", now knows it is a window for Creation, allowing it to experience itself in all its fullness and glory.

Thinking is a tool used for enlightenment and the transfer of information, but it can become a crutch if it is not easily released when not necessary. It is already a part of the veil used by Creation to limit itself, so using it to eliminate the veil can be tricky. Even the highest thought of all – "I am not my thoughts," or "These thoughts are not mine," must be used with care. It is much better to dive into the feeling of "I" within. Let the electrical connection or chemical bond created by each thought, the bond binding Consciousness to the body identity, dissolve when thought ceases producing the chemical.

Feel the Self within instead of listening to thoughts about the self or about what you are not. Know there is no higher thought than thoughtlessness, no more usefulness for the mind than to be free of thought. This allows mind to expand and use the energy of thought to experience Consciousness, to be in the here and now, and to live in this moment, conscious of the input of the senses, the environment, and of Creation all around.

Once the Universe decides it is your time to be enlightened, there is nothing that you can do to stop it from happening. We are all being pulled, like water swirling down the drain; it will happen to all of us, and it is just a matter of time. In the meantime, the impatient mind wants all the answers now, wants to feel the end of the push and pull of opposites, and of course wants to know freedom before dinner time.

That is what books like this are for. If the universe intends for the person to know their true identity quickly, they will read something in this or another book and it will click and the moment of enlightenment has occurred. If the Universe intends for the process to be slower, the aspirant will be given a propensity to study a particular path. This study will eventually lead to the moment when the Universe has gathered all the information into the particular mind it has chosen for this particular type of enlightenment, and the final piece of knowledge will take the person from the old understanding to the new one.

For some there will be the knowledge that there is more, the belief that they want to know more, but there will be enough resistance to the knowledge as to prevent the understanding from taking root, or for learning to occur. What is happening on the grander scale is nothing more than the Universe has decided that it wants to feel yearning through one of its parts, a yearning that will continue on for some time without being quenched. This is the drama it has chosen, and a particular person is gifted with the privilege of playing that part. When the Universe is finished with that particular feeling from that particular role, the Universe moves on to a different feeling for that character, be it forgetting about the spiritual path for now, or the release of beliefs that stood in the way of enlightenment.

Releasing the many beliefs we have grown accustomed to, not the least of which is the "I am my body and my mind" belief is not an easy task. It really only happens when the Universe/Creation decides it is ready for itself playing the particular person to believe something new.

From the person perspective you have finally gotten enough evidence to believe something different from your previous belief. You finally have a change in the connections in your neural-holographic skull and can see a certain teaching now appears true for you. The teaching hasn't changed, but your relationship to it has. It makes sense to you now, whereas previously it was foolishness or incomprehensible.

In other words, you have become ready, you have enough belief and knowledge that the next piece seems to fit in with what you have. Or what actually happens is the next piece unlocks the potentiality that was always awaiting within you to understanding, and the process of your enlightenment moment can proceed until the time that the final piece is revealed on the outside and mirrored on the inside as understanding.

Attaining realization is a very straightforward process, but it can appear to be a cosmic mystery if you don't understand how it works. It can be termed "Grace", and for some, that term is enough. If we choose to look deeply enough inside of it, we can see it has many moving parts which all work together to create the magic.

Stars are what Creation uses to create planets and sustain life on them; minds are what the universe uses on this level of existence to observe, experience, think and eventually enlighten.

Chapter Nineteen: Why the Mystique to Enlightenment?

What is it that is mysteriously transferred from master to student? Why do we need to believe something so magical is transmitted? Some schools of thought will say things like, "The Master will awaken the disciple with a touch, a look or even by their will." As a seeker I believed this to be the case, and I was not alone in my belief.

Fortunately I did not hold onto this belief blindly, but instead I followed it as deeply as I could. I realized if this was a true statement, then there was indeed a transfer of some type happening. Either there was some mysterious power that the Master was aware of and can control that he passes to the student – like a wizard pointing a magic wand and electric bolts coming out directed at the disciple- or some other transmission was occurring.

I contemplated long and hard on this subject and then, finally, the light came on. The way most of humanity transfers ideas and concepts from one another is the same way that Masters transfer spiritual knowledge and awakening: through words!

Why the human mind makes it so mysterious must be so that there can be a higher level of acceptance. Receptivity is always increased when there is belief on the side of the believer. If I were to say to you, "The master is going to tell you this and you will hear it and understand it," you may believe and listen, or you might not. If instead I said, "The Master will bestow Grace upon you and transmit this highest teaching directly into your heart," as a seeker you would rejoice knowing you were about to receive a gift of great value. The more pomp and ceremony that surrounds the transfer of information, the more the human mind tends to accept it and the higher the value the mind gives to it.

This book could contain the essence of the highest teachings of the Self, but if it were free, very few would value it. If all one needed to do to become enlightened was to pick up a pebble on the side of a road, very few would believe this to be possible and fewer still would actually do it. If instead we said the famed "Enlightenment Stone" had been enlivened by the ancient Master fifty centuries ago and was placed in a special divine location and if you made a large offering in the name of the stone and then traveled to touch it you were guaranteed enlightenment within seven years, many more people would make a pilgrimage to a pebble to pick it up and many of those who did would eventually become enlightened.

The higher the value we place on something and the more mystery we shroud it in, the more the subconscious can believe in it, and the more this belief can shape our experience of the world toward the goal of the mysterious object. Knowing this, maybe we can circumvent this subconscious need and take the conscious mind straight to the goal. Or maybe we can focus the conscious mind on a goal with enough fervor and intention so as to make the subconscious follow our will.

We did this every day when we learned something new at school; we can use this same process to learn this simple understanding that is enlightenment too. The need for complexity has its place when we do not understand it, but once we know why ceremony and mystery are used, they lose their exclusive hold on our inner world, and enable us to use other means to achieve the same goal.

A similar peculiarity can be observed when observing experience: you value most the experiences you learn firsthand. Too few of us are able to learn from other's mistakes. We value and believe something when we do it, as opposed to when someone else does it and tells us about it.

This stems from the same factor as ceremony. Our minds are set up to believe most when they see it. If they are told it, there is a lower acceptance of it as being true and applicable, so we need to go through it ourselves in order for it to really mean something, and in order to truly learn it. This "doing" is what takes learning to its deepest level. You can be told, "Don't touch the stove because it is hot," a million times, but it only takes one time burning your fingers for you to learn not to put them on a hot stove.

So the mystique surrounding enlightenment serves several purposes. It turns the casual seeker away from consciously wanting the experience. It is the gatekeeper making sure only the serious student passes through to the path of enlightenment. Then it makes those few who do pass believe they are special, and that what they are doing is unique, and that although the path is difficult, they are worthy enough to tread it. For those who can finally break through to the goal, the mystique can serve as a force of change in the subconscious, a force that allows the mind to believe it is receiving great knowledge and understanding and is moving towards the goal. The mystique basically lets the mind believe it is becoming enlightened. It is only once the final light comes on when the former seeker can begin to understand the tools that brought about enlightenment.

When we can bring our understanding of the power of the mystique together with the way the mind works, we can use one-pointed focus to put the goal of enlightenment into the subconscious, much as the mystique did before. We can believe the experiences of other like-minded seekers and trust the tips they give us on the road to enlightenment.

We can then choose to walk a much faster path to the enlightenment, not burdened by mystery and the need to make every mistake and wrong turn before eventually reaching realization. Instead our load is light, our path short, and our journey sweet.

Chapter Twenty: Final Words for Awakening Your New Understanding

So what if you have reached this point and still don't get it? One thing we need to realize is that most teachings are not just keys that fit the lock that is your understanding. Teachings can be seen as keys, but you are much more a locksmith than you may believe.

You have the ability to take a key that is pretty close to what you need to unlock your understanding and file a little here and weld just a touch there to adjust the shape of the key to fit your needs. When a teaching has almost everything you need to understand it, you can use other teachings to fill in the personal lacking you feel to better understand it. At the end of each one of our lives, we will all have a philosophy that is unique to one. It is a patchwork, hopefully a beautiful one that has guided you to a space in which you are satisfied. You hold many tenets from one teacher and a few like ones from another and still others from the experiences of your life. All rolled together it is your philosophy, one that you would teach to a class of eager students, some of whom would get it all and add only a few things to it and others of whom would take most of it and leave a few thoughts that you might feel are very critical.

Of course I have done just that in this writing, taking what I felt was the best and most useful of the teachings that took me to enlightenment - and left me without a "me" to be enlightened. The ashram and the books and my studies obviously contained a lot of other things, things that I winnowed out as not pertinent to getting me to my goal. Things like the worship that some do to a Guru, the inner spiritual visions and sounds I experienced, and the human frailties of teachers of which I have known, to name a few were possible detours along my path, but ones on which I did not dally long. They did not move me forward on my path, although too many seekers find themselves either sidetracked or altogether derailed by these things. For me it was always a matter of staying focused on the goal, sometimes because and at other times in spite of the teachings I was following.

If a teaching has something, one thing that is just too outrageous for you to take, "A book on non-duality that mentions aliens beings! Ha," a voice reading this book may say. Many a Guru has lost droves of disciples on a valid path only because of strange idiosyncrasies. Not to imply that there are not valid reasons to leave a Guru or that a path needs to be sanitized before it can teach a student anything. Only that each of us, as students to the Guru that is the world, have eyes that we can use to discern teachings in the most unlikely of places and situations, when we choose to do so.

Everything can teach something, if we are open to learning. I have sat in very fundamental churches, or spoken with people with very conservative thoughts, and walked away learning something from them that aided me on my path. Even if what I learned was not what they thought they were teaching, and even if what I got from them would have appalled them to know they gave me, I still was able to garner something from an interaction starting only with the point of view that I could learn from the situation. When we approach teachings and life in general with a mind open to learning instead of with a mind intend on finding the faults, we usually are surprised at how much useful information we can get.

So now let's examine what the probable reasons could be if you still have not imbibed this teaching on enlightenment. Any one of these may be what is holding you back, or a combination of them.

1) You cannot let go of the thought, "I am my body and my mind."

This belief is undoubtedly the single largest stumbling block to enlightenment. From birth we are aware of senses that are seemingly attached to the body. We hear thoughts from an early age that appear to come from inside the mind, and everyone around us interacts with us as if we were an individual, just as they believe themselves to be. We are taught to use the word "I" when talking about ourselves, and by the age of two or three it finally kicks in fully, "I am a person!" From then on, this belief only flourishes, based on the observation of the senses. It is reinforced by a society of others who have done the same and assumed the belief inherited from their forefathers and predecessors was the correct way to see the world.

Throughout your life, there is no input to the contrary and everything you encounter actually further solidifies this belief. To think otherwise only seems crazy, if you get right down to it. It is easy to disregard the few mystics and who have experienced themselves as being more than just their bodies, and it is easy enough to dismiss the people who leave their bodies and experience living beyond them, either through out of body experiences or near death experiences. As long as you or your neighbor or your mother or father, or the guy sitting next to you Sunday, either in church or on the couch watching football do not believe it, then you figure, "This isn't something I'm gonna believe either".

If I were trying to persuade you not that you are not your body, but that your body and mind do not really live in an exterior world, or that your body and mind were really just holographic images, you would more than likely still not believe, but the sensory proof for the former hypothesis only proves it, and the scientific proof for the latter is building by the day and being tested by scientists at this very moment. We are very used to thinking we have a solid, material body in a material world, but the deeper science goes in examining this, just like the exploration of the flat earth, when they look at it, it may not conform to previous beliefs and assumptions.

When we get right down to an examination of the body and the world which is done tremendously by Rupert Spira in *The Transparency of Things*, we can see every single thought we have about our bodies and our world around them is wrong.

Throughout history mankind has done nothing but assume. When Western technology caught up to the needs of a worldwide civilization, expeditions were launched to better understand the shape of the world. Now that Western science is catching up to the realities of the inner world of the body, it shows a picture much different than what was previously assumed. We see that the brain is the sole processor of the senses, and these inputs are actually the only ones that show us anything outside of our consciousness, which includes all of the body and the world. When we understand that all of our experiences are processed by the brain, we see that our world is only happening on a screen in the brain. All of the rest is projection and assumption.

For many of us to even consider this is too ground shaking; to let go of who we thought we were leaves us with nothing, and even realization isn't worth it. Which is fine, although ultimately when Creation decides it is your time to know your Self, it will give you the experience to shake loose your incorrect but tightly held belief in being the body.

I was lucky since Creation gave me an experience I yearned for, an awakening experience that showed me in no uncertain terms what was real and what was not. Experiencing my awareness beyond the confines of my body and having the feeling that this was a very familiar experience eliminated any question of my being just the body and mind. On top of that was the feeling that this awareness was truly natural and basic, and that I was experiencing being awake consciously for the first time. On top of all of that, the inner admonishment of "How could I ever have thought that I was just this little body," cemented for me the fact that my mind had fairly recently forgotten a truth that I had known long before, and I was being reminded of the truth of existence.

Whether the cause of this experience was chemicals in my body, or spirit guides, or alien entities, or the Guru's grace or the Universe itself, is immaterial. The fact is that the ultimate cause was the entirety of the Universe, deciding now was the time to bring this particular part of itself into knowledge of itself, and this was the latest, most powerful step it would take on the path to my enlightenment.

In my book *How to Become Enlightened in 12 Days,* the goal is to give you the understanding that I had and to show you 12 techniques to expand your consciousness beyond your body. If you are able to really get into just one of the exercises or games, you can begin to have an experience of how much greater than the body you really are. If you can experience for a moment that you are more than your body, as the practices I spoke about earlier let you eventually do, you will be able to let go of this hurdle. If you could just believe you existed beyond the confines of the body, believing you were more and understanding the truth would be a lot easier.

Just because you have believed something for your entire life, doesn't make it true. Examination, true seeing and feeling, and discernment are all necessary to experience what is real beyond what these basic senses we have access to tell us.

-----

2) You don't believe you are your body, but you do believe, "I am a soul living life through my body."

The belief that you are a soul or that you have a spirit and that this is what inhabits the body should not be a large stepping stone to believing that you are much greater than your body. To believe that you are some non-corporeal being already says that you are not your body. It says you are not your brain. It says you believe yourself to be an individual entity that moved into a material home for a short duration of time known as "life" and that you will move on when that time is done. Maybe you believe you are here to learn things during your stay, or to love and do good things for others. You might even believe you will do it again in order to get it right, or that you will be rewarded for your good works with an eternal pass to heaven.

These beliefs are not so different from what you need to understand in order to experience enlightenment, but the big difference is the belief in an individual doer. Whether it be a body, a mind or a soul, believing you are one separate from all others in an immense ocean of others is not quite the best way to see things. If you are a soul, are you a soul with limits to your size? Can you feel where your soul ends and another begins? Is it the concept of soul that you are attached to, or is it the personality of who you believe yourself to be that you most love? Look at your answers to each of these questions. See deeply what you really believe about yourself.

More than likely you will end up with the belief that you are an individual something of indeterminate, finite size that will live forever. If you look at this, you can immediately see that being an individual is the single belief that keeps you from accepting enlightenment and is now what you believe in most, and you find any teaching to the contrary has got to be wrong.

Understanding what is meant by the term individual can help. If you mean a mind that thinks, how can we prove that thoughts originate in the mind? Our minds can just as easily be receivers for thought that comes from a central location as they can be the originator of each thought. There is no need for an individual for thought to occur as we know it. There is actually interesting scientific experimentation on this very topic, and the conclusions point in the direction of thought not working in the ways we have traditionally assumed.

If you believe individual means having choice and free will, see 3) below.

3) "I believe I am an individual with choice and free will."

If you believe you have choice, can you choose not to think for more than a few moments? Can you choose not to breathe? Can you choose to be still for an hour or two? Do you have the free will to concentrate your thought on a particular object for 30 minutes or an hour without it moving? Do you have the free will to get on an airplane and go halfway around the world tonight? As you can see, choice and free will are easy to believe in, but proving you have them is not easy. Most people cannot do all of the things I ask above. If you look at the questions above, you see some point to the fact that we are not separate from the world, but are inseparably linked to one another and the demands of the world. The bodies we experience need air. We have no free will or choice to believe otherwise. Yogi's will also tell you that you need prana, which connects you to the energy of the universe. All of this says you may have the illusion of separateness, but it is only an illusion that when seen more clearly shows that we are all part of a whole, all tied to one another. How many countless others conspire together with you to be able to get on a plane and travel halfway around the world tonight? If you really have the will power you believed you had, you could still your mind for a couple of hours right now and know for sure whether any of this was true or not.

So let go of the false belief that you are an island who can do everything on his or her own simply by choosing. As science has theorized for some time now, having come from a "Big Bang" a moment of immense entanglement of particles, once this universe expanded, the entanglements did not stop. Quantum physics shows that once a particle has a connection to another, it always has that connection, and although we are larger than the quantum world, we find ourselves still bound in this way.

In a holographic environment this understanding only increases as it says that each point contains the whole, so we are inextricably linked, which is the exact opposite of an individual with a will separate from the whole.

-----

4) "If this is true, then why doesn't everyone know it already?"

Just because everyone didn't know the sun revolved around the earth didn't make it any less true. Same for the round world, same for germ theory... the list goes on into history. There has been and will always be a new, better explanation for why the world is at it appears. When we see anything, humanity immediately describes it in terms that it knows. In the times that humanity becomes wiser, when more information is available, descriptions are modified. If a belief is held for a short period of time by but a few people, it is easier to change than if it is held by a lot of people for a long time.

This is the nature of people and knowledge. It does not make sense to most of us that an explanation should change. In this present moment we find our minds experiencing, we believe we are the most sophisticated beings, with the most knowledge, and any possible evidence to the contrary is easy to dismiss.

These days we are exposed to more and more credible people who tell us they are in contact with non-humans, be it in the form of non-corporeal channeled entities or alien beings. The information these beings share tell humans that we are not necessarily at the top of the intellectual ladder. Some say the entities or beings are here to help us grow, but as long as those of us not listening to them hold onto the belief that we already know all that we need to know, there will not be an openness to their teachings, or even to the possibility that these teachings exist.

Ultimately, the experience of enlightenment is inherent in all true teachings. The feeling of Being within cannot be synthesized and transcends all schools of thought, even possible non-human ones!

At each moment in history a majority of people believed in the same way, from those who thought gods in the sky controlled the elements of nature, to those who believed Newtonian physics explained the workings of the physical world perfectly, to those who believed they lived in the "end times' when god was going to send plagues to end the world.

The truth is that we do not really understand even a small fraction of reality, and what is a laughable theory today will be a scientific fact a hundred years from now and an unfortunate example of scientific ignorance five hundred years from now. Understanding on all fronts is always expanding, and this is definitely the case with our experience of life.

We must be open to being pioneers, ready to move forward if there is enough evidence in favor of a new paradigm. Just because everyone doesn't believe it today doesn't negate its veracity. If we are looking for the institutions of our current society to do anything other than sustain themselves, we will be sadly disappointed. We must instead look to ourselves, to our experiences, to our intuition and feel what is right for us to investigate.

We are all part of the whole and at the particular point that is experiencing "you" at this moment, there is no better or more connected example for the Universe to choose. The "you" you believe you are is the best in your realm, the one and only connection the Universe uses for all the disparate pieces of information you hold, and the Universe will use "you" to know itself when the connections and information reach a critical mass. It will not wait for all the others to become enlightened, then give you the experience.

This is true if only because these teachings are not available to the mass of people yet, and the mass of people are not open to them, yet. So if you have made it to this point, there is enough resonance in you to allow you to believe enough to try on a new understanding, before everyone else.

-----

5) "I cannot teach my subconscious to hold this understanding. I need mystery, ceremony and a mystique to surround the understanding before I can accept it."

After all of this writing, all I can say to this, final misunderstanding is, "For an outrageous sum of money – large enough to make you really believe this is invaluable information - I will be happy to invite you to attend a two-day course I will be holding in the near future!"

Seriously, don't let your long held and unfounded beliefs stand in the way of your enlightenment. All you need to understand it is here, all you need to experience it is here. Reread for a deeper understanding, and let your walls of resistance fall away.

Or you can use any one of the many great books I have referenced herein and delve deeply into what is holding you back. Or you can decide to dive into one or more of the practices described in the previous pages.

There really is nothing more for you to learn.

At best, all of this may be said in a different manner that can resonate with you on a deeper level and be Creation's way of saying, "Now is my time through you."

If that is what you need, again I say… "I will be happy to invite you to attend a two-day course I will be holding in the near future!"

Why do we search for this experience of Self? Inherent in our minds, which are the link to Awareness, is the yearning for Peace, Bliss and Love. All are but facets of the same feeling of completion, and we have an inner drive to feel these experiences in our lives as much as possible. The things we fill our lives with try to satisfy this craving, but they fall short. When we believe the next rollercoaster ride is going to satisfy us, the best we find is that in a moment or two during the ride, we were present in this moment, not thinking about doing something else, not worried about needing something else. We were present and focused on what was happening and we were actually living in the moment which we were experiencing.

When we are living in this moment, which really means when we are not lost in thought at a particular moment but actually in touch with what our senses are providing us, when we are enjoying and reacting to this stimulus, then we are truly alive. Otherwise we are inside of the book of our lives, watching words and experiencing symbols which the mind uses to always try to categorize and judge everything life.

This activity of the mind never actually touches the fabric that is real life. Living may seem simple enough, but very few people really immerse themselves in it. Instead they think about living, lost in the next thought as life passes them by.

Realization allows us to see life in a manner that does not value thinking so much anymore. It allows us to see ourselves as more than the thinking apparatus many of us were at one time so proud of. It allows us to know that there is an experience beyond thought, and a way to live that values experience over words, and being over figuring out what we should be doing. It brings a calm to the mind and allows it to stop worrying so much, which in turn allows it to stop its incessant thinking and allow life to proceed without the need to orchestrate each moment in fear that it will not turn out the way we believe it must.

Life is grand enough to take care of itself; it does not need a little body and mind to direct it on its path. When we learn this to be true, life can take on a different flavor and have a more enjoyable tone than ever before. The sound of one hand clapping becomes your immediate motion instead of an opportunity for more mental gymnastics. You witness what occurs, not mistakenly believing you are making it happen.

A lightness for life itself results when you have this approach to the moments of your day. The only thing life awaits is for you to recognize and realize that *your* self actually is *the* Self.

Reading List

*I Am That, Nisargadatta Maharaj translated by Maurice Frydman

*Awakening to the Dream, Leo Hartong

*The Concise Yoga Vasistha, Swami Venkatesananda

*Who Am I, Ramana Maharshi

*Prior to Consciousness, Nisargadatta Maharaj edited by Jean Dunn

*The Transparency of Things, Rupert Spira

*Zen Mind, Beginner's Mind, Shunryu Suzuki

*How to Become Enlightened in 12 Days, G. Tyler Wright

In Search of the Miraculous, P. D. Ouspensky

Think on These Things, J. Krishnamurti

The Mystique of Enlightenment, U. G. Krishnamurti

Instant ESP, David St. Clair

Silva Mind Control, Jose Silva

The Science of Mind, Ernest Holmes

Autobiography of a Yogi, Paramahansa Yogananda

Creative Visualization, Shakti Gowain

The Gnostic Gospels, Elaine Pagels

I Have Become Alive, Swami Muktananda

Play of Consciousness, Swami Muktananda

Light on Pranayama, B. K. Iyengar

Power of Now, Eckhart Tolle

The Holographic Universe, Michael Talbot

The Doctrine of Recognition, Ksemaraja, translated
by Jaideva Singh

*Highly recommended

If you liked this book, tell a friend, write a review and read

other recommended titles which can be found at

TranscendentWritings.com

Non Fiction:

How to Become Enlightened in 12 Days by G. Tyler Wright

How to Transform Your Life in 9 Days: Awakening and Living

Your Life Connected to Being by G. Tyler Wright

Three Easy Steps to Enlightenment: Essential Inner Shifts for

Realizing the Self by G. Tyler Wright

Source Energy Speaks: A Conversation with the Creative

Aspect of Being by G. Tyler Wright

The Happy Mom's Guide: Reducing Stress in Your Life- 10 Days

to Freedom by G. Tyler Wright

How to Find Your Royal Ancestry for Free in Less Than 14 Days

by Gregory Wright

Transcendent Fiction:

The first full length novel in the Gray Soul Saga

Secret Soulmates: A Spiritual Journey of Love and Discovery by Gregory Wright

The Game's On: Play to Stay Alive by Gregory Wright

Parallel Love by Gregory Wright

Alarm Yourself by Gregory Wright

Beware the Haze in the Distance by Greg Wright

Surfin' to the End of the World by Greg Wright

Golden Prophecy: Prelude to the Gray Soul Saga by Gregory Wright

Enlightenment Now

TranscendentWritings.com

Printed in Great Britain
by Amazon

44143075R00156